Tutankhamun's Egypt

Cyril Aldred

Charles Scribner's Sons • New York

Acknowledgement is due to the following for permission to reproduce illustrations (colour plates are referred to in Roman numerals) : Ägyptisches Museum, Berlin, 60; Ashmolean Museum, 9, 11, 17, 72, 76, 78, 79; British Museum, 6, 7, 74; Brooklyn Museum, 38; Peter Clayton, 32, 57; Egypt Exploration Society, 14, 16, 53; Hirmer Archives, 4, 12, 21, 24, 25, 26, 37, 45, 54, 61, 75; Michael Holford, V, VI, VIII; © F. L. Kenett, 13, 15, 18, 35, 46, 55, 66; Mansell Collection, 27; Marburg, 22, 41, 42, 44, 77; Tom Scott, 2, 3, 10, 19, 57, 63; Staatliche Museum, Berlin, 47; Roger Viollet, 28; John Webb, cover and title page, 5, 8, 39, 51, 67, IV; ZFA, II, III.

The map on page 4 was drawn by Nigel Holmes and the Chronology on page 6 compiled by Paul Jordan.

The illustration on the front cover shows mourners at the burial of the Vizier Ramose (detail of plate V). The wife is supported by an attendant. Their garments are ungirt, they pour dust on their heads while tears course down their cheeks. 'The great shepherd departs,' they wail. 'He passes by us! Come, return unto us!'

3 5 7 9 11 13 15 17 19 Q/P 20 18 16 14 12 10 8 6 4 2

Printed in the United States of America
Library of Congress Catalog Card Number 78-50841
ISBN 0-684-15795-0

Contents

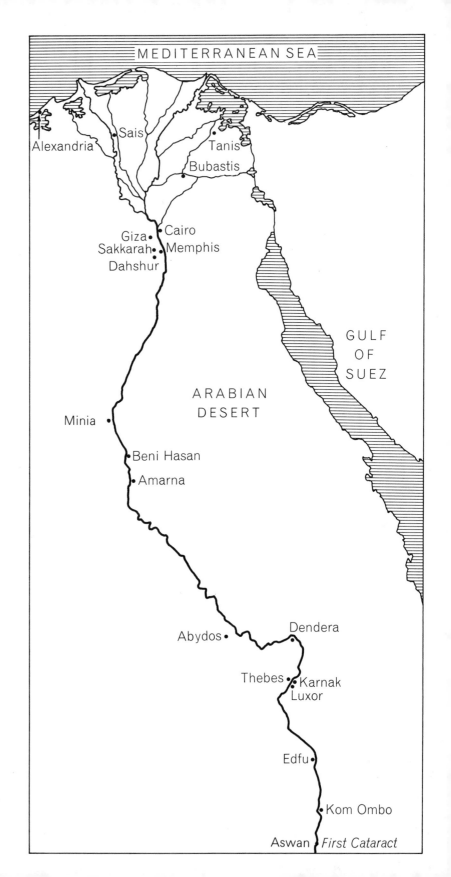

Introduction

When the boy Tut-ankh-amun came to the throne of his ancestors about the year 1362 BC, Egypt had already existed as a kingdom for over 1700 years with a characteristic culture which, however, had adapted itself to the changed conditions of the Late Bronze Age. The great stone pyramids of Giza, Sakkarah and Dahshur had by then fallen into ruins, their mortuary cults had lapsed and they were visited only by sightseers looking at the past. In a song which the young king must have heard, the poet pointed to them as examples of the vanity of human aspirations as he exhorted his listeners to eat, drink and be merry, for tomorrow death would come to them, too.

Such moralisings did not prevent the Egyptians from burying their Pharaoh with a wealth of treasure which, when it was found virtually intact in 1922, did nothing to dispel that aura of sensational mystery and exotic obscurity that has always surrounded the Ancient Egyptians from Classical times right down to the Romantic Age in which they were re-discovered. Many of the hoary old misconceptions still remain. In the following chapters, as in the television programmes on which they are based, the aim has been to show the Ancient Egyptians as a people trying to grapple with the problems of living in the world of the century in which Tut-ankh-amun reigned.

Chronology

	This is the period when the foundations of Egyptian civilisation were laid. Egypt was not at this time a united country. It was only at the close of this period that Narmer, a king of Upper (Southern) Egypt, united the 'Two Lands'. An interesting King of Upper Egypt in late predynastic times was the 'Scorpion King'.
	The First Dynasty of the newly-united country was founded, according to tradition, by Menes, whom archaeologists identify with King Narmer.
	Imhotep built the 'Step Pyramid' for King Djoser. This was the great age of pyramid building. Cheops and Chephren are among its famous kings, Hemon and Ankhaf among its architects. The splendid statues of Prince Rahotep and his wife belong to this time.
	A time when the power of the great nobles was beginning to grow at the expense of the King's. The lavishly appointed tomb of Mereruka at Sakkarah belongs to this time. After the long rule of the last Pharaoh of this dynasty, Pepy II, internal strife led to the complete breakdown of national government.
	During this troubled feudal period, with its ephemeral and local dynasties, pyramids and tombs were ransacked.

THE MIDDLE KINGDOM 11th Dynasty 2133–1991	Egypt was gradually brought back under unified rule. Mentuhotep II centred his new government on Thebes. The Governor Mesehti took to his grave two sets of wooden model soldiers.
12th Dynasty 1991–1786	A period of strong central rule, under the powerful Sesostrid pharaohs. A jar of Nile water from the tomb of Sit-Hathor Yunet belongs to this time.

2ND INTERMEDIATE PERIOD 13th–17th Dynasties 1786–1567	A confused period, dominated in its latter half by foreign (Hyksos) rule, especially in Lower (Northern) Egypt.

THE NEW KINGDOM 18th Dynasty 1567–1320	The kings of this dynasty, the first of whom expelled the foreign rulers, were among the most powerful and celebrated of all the pharaohs of Ancient Egypt. Among them, Amenophis I, II, and III; Queen Hatshepsut; Tuthmosis III; Tuthmosis IV; Akhenaten and Tut-ankh-amun. The jewellery of Queen Ah-hotep and the splendid tombs of the nobles at Thebes belonged to this period. Rekhmire was a great vizier of the time, and Amenophis-son-of-Hapu raised the Colossi of Memnon for Amenophis III.
19th and 20th Dynasties 1320–1085	During these two dynasties, Egyptian imperial power went from its zenith under Seti I and Ramesses II into decline under the later Ramessids, when the Asiatic dependencies were lost and another bout of tomb-looting began.

THE LATE DYNASTIC PERIOD 21st–30th Dynasties 1085–341	A succession of foreign rulers interleaved with native Egyptian pharaohs oversaw Ancient Egypt's final decline. The last real Egyptian pharaoh was Nectanebo II, who built extensively all over Egypt until driven out of power by the Persians.

THE PTOLEMAIC PERIOD 332–30	During this period of rule by the descendants of Alexander's general, the great temples of Philae, Edfu, Kom Ombo, Esna and Dendera were built.

I

Scene in the tomb-chamber of the craftsman Snedjem at Deir el-Medina, Western Thebes, showing the owner and his wife performing agricultural labours in the Fields of Yalu – the Egyptian equivalent of the Elysian fields. Like Egypt, this Netherworld, ruled by Osiris, has its fields, canals, ponds, and groves of date and dom palms and its flowering plants. The Egyptian farmer could readily visualise Paradise as a land where perpetual spring prevailed and the corn grew to a height of nine cubits. The good life consisted in tending the domains of Osiris eternally as he had once cultivated the fields of Egypt.

1 The People

For the most part the Ancient Egyptians, like their descendants today, were farmers laboriously tilling the soil of Egypt, draining its marshlands and extending the cultivation little by little every year. The development of their natural resources was the constant preoccupation of countless generations who boasted of the produce of their fields and were no less proud of their prize cattle fattened and garlanded for sacrifice to the gods, or for display on the day they were counted for census purposes.

The power and prestige of Ancient Egypt reposed mainly in its agriculture, and in this respect it was the wealthiest country in the ancient world, though its immense gold reserves and monopoly of tropical products made it esteemed and courted by the other great nations of antiquity. Nevertheless it was its fleshpots that were celebrated among the contiguous hungry nations, its surplus grain succouring the Hittites in their days of famine as well as the city mob a millennium later in the time of Imperial Rome.

Here is how the poet Paibes described the great city of Raamses on the building of which in the thirteenth century BC the Israelites were supposed to have toiled:

Its fields are full of all good things and it has provisions and sustenance every day. Its channels abound in fish and its lakes in birds. Its plots are green with herbage and its banks bear dates. Its granaries are overflowing with barley and wheat and they reach unto the sky. Fruits and fish are there for sustenance and wine from the vineyards of Kankeme surpassing honey. He who dwells there is happy: and there the humble man is like the great elsewhere.

For the Ancient Egyptians were a greatly privileged community inhabiting a rainless land that straggled a long narrow oasis for hundreds of miles in the African deserts but was blessed with a prodigious fertility. It was independent of the caprice of the weather for its prosperity and in favoured localities could bring forth two crops each year.

For most of its length, the Egyptian looking across the Nile could see the boundaries of his world in the rich mud that was deposited each year by the inundation of the great river. Beyond this narrow fertile belt was tawny desert, mostly sterile and inhospitable. The division between cultivation and aridity, life and death, good and evil, was therefore clear and complete and gave the Egyptian his characteristic awareness of an essential duality in his universe.

The Ancient Egyptian believed that the waters that were under the earth welled up each year from subterranean caverns and submerged the land in their flood. To this simple circumstance Egypt owed her fertility, indeed her very existence and the character of her ancient civilisation. Except at rare intervals when a succession of low Niles brought 'the years of the hyaena when men went hungry', or when too high a flood destroyed the ancient protective dams and dykes, the beneficent river spread its life-giving waters and fertilising mud over the exhausted land in an annual miracle of rebirth out of aridity. In the semi-tropical climate abundant crops could be rapidly produced each season and an ample surplus was available for next year's seed and for lean times.

The farmer's labours, though well rewarded, were burdensome and almost continuous except at the height of the inundation. They were largely concerned with irrigation, with the raising of dams to hold back flood-water in shallow basins so that silt could settle on the fields and the ground become thoroughly soaked; or the piercing of dykes to allow water to flow from one area to another as the river receded; or the building of moles to protect towns from the flood-waters. In spring and summer the higher-lying fields had to be watered by means of the *shaduf* or well-sweep, or from jars suspended from a yoke.

Besides its arable farms, Egypt had a large population of domestic animals such as oxen, sheep, goats, pigs and donkeys, and later the horse. The cattle-breeders and herdsmen led a freer and more nomadic existence in the natural habitat of such animals, the marshlands, particularly those of the Delta with their lush pasturage and thickets of rush. But the vast majority of the Egyptians were committed to the cultivation of land as much by predilection as of necessity. They were deeply attached to the soil and un-happy away from their valley.

They did not, however, function spontaneously but had to be organised and directed on a national scale so that the gifts of the Nile could be developed to the full. They were merely the governed. In our next chapters we shall look at the men who governed them.

2

To the right above, the scribe Nakht sits in an arbour watching with a benevolent eye the work in his fields. Before him are sacks of corn and a meal of dates, bread, onions and wine. A farmer guides his plough pulled by two heifers which are yoked at the horns. Other labourers fell trees or hack at scrub. Below, a farmer and his men plough and seed the fresh earth. On the higher ground the inundation has left pools and mud in which the hoers sink to their ankles. A thirsty worker takes a pull from a water-skin slung in a tree.

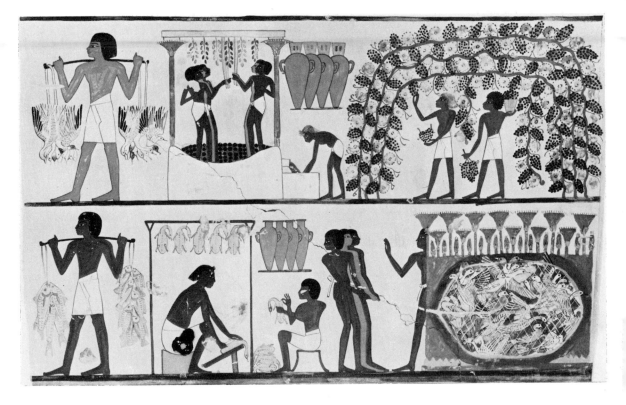

3 (above)

In the upper register grapes are picked from vines grown espalier-wise, and brought to the press where five men tread them out. The wine gushing forth is bottled in large amphorae closed with a rush and mud cap and stamped with an oval seal. Below, three men at a signal given by the look-out in the papyrus thicket are trapping fowl over a pool set with a clap-net. Two men are plucking, cleaning and 'jerking' the birds before preserving them in jars with salt. Offering-bearers bring pomegranates, birds, grapes and fish.

4 (left above)

Userhet in his chariot hunts gazelles, hares and other creatures of the desert. A pair of hyaenas have been flushed out; one flees with the rest, the other sinks wounded. The desert wadys in ancient times had not been reduced to complete aridity by over-grazing by goats and camels. They supported wild game, ibex, gazelles, ostriches, hares and their predators, the lion and his relations. Userhet is shown in the usual convention of dashing into the chase, either of men or animals, with the reins tied round his waist. Actually, he would be driven by a groom.

5 (left below)

A scribe, right, registers the tropical products brought from Nubia and the Sudan. In the upper row, these consist of logs of ebony, ostrich feathers, a basket of ostrich eggs, gold in the form of rings and bags of dust, a green monkey on its special stool and six jars of ochre. In the lower register, besides gold of various grades, there are cheetah skins, elephant tusks and baskets of carnelians and green-stone. The ivory and ebony were exported in finished products all over the Near East. Both names in fact reflect their ancient Egyptian origins.

6 (above)

Farmers delivering their cattle for an annual count and tax assessment. If an animal had died, its hide had to be produced instead. The scribes on the left with their document chests and writing cases are entering numbers and checking inventories. A farmer, above, kneels to greet the chief accountant, kissing his foot. The cattleman with the rolled halter calls out to his companion: 'Buck up! Don't natter to the effendi. He detests blitherers. He'll do what is right and won't listen to your tale. He records the silent man properly and is not hard on folk. He knows what's what.'

7 (right)

Offering-tables piled high with some of the produce of Egyptian farms. On the left is an ornamental bouquet made of papyrus stalks, lotus flowers and mandrake fruits. In the foreground are four wine-jars on light wicker stands draped with vine leaves and floral caps. Such jars were inscribed with the year of vintage, the names of the vineyard and vintner, and often the assessment of quality. Behind them is a rush mat heaped with loaves and cakes, honeycomb, baskets of figs, pomegranates, bunches of grapes, cuts of beef, a goose and a bunch of lotus flowers.

8 (above)

The Egyptians personified the Nile as Hapy, a fat, well-fed denizen of the marshlands, often painted blue and bearing gifts including jars of water, river plants, pond-fowl and fish. The waters of the Nile, which could turn desert into fertile land, were thought to be charged with divine power able to create life out of death. A hymn to Hapy describes him as 'The Father of the Gods, Abundance . . . the Food of Egypt. Everyone rejoices on the day you come forth from your cavern,' – a reference to the annual inundation of the Nile.

9 (right)

At each inundation all the able-bodied men were called up for service in the national corvée when the peasantry were thrown out of work by the rising waters of the Nile. They reported for duty with their earth-moving equipment – a hoe, pick and basket – with which they cleared irrigation channels and raised dykes. A similar compulsory service was thought to exist in the Osirian Hereafter, and the Egyptian provided himself with magic substitutes, *shawabti* figures, which would perform such onerous labours for him. Even kings were not exempt and this shawabti of Tut-ankh-amun is one of many that were buried with him.

10

A scene in the tomb of Ipy shows the house of the owner, left, with steps leading up to the portico. The garden is being watered by a hunch-back working at a *shaduf* or well-sweep. A leather bucket on the end of a pole is counterbalanced by a mass of limestone at the other end. The pole pivots on a support of whitewashed mud. With such a device the Egyptian watered his high-lying fields during the summer cultivation. The machine is still used in rural areas of Egypt. The garden grows papyrus, lotus, cornflowers, poppy, mandrakes, pomegranates, willow, persea and figs.

2   The Divine King

While Egypt may have been the gift of the Nile, as the Greeks affirmed, the peculiar nature of its culture was the creation of their Pharaohs. Civilisation arose in river valleys elsewhere in the Near East with economies based upon agriculture: they, too, had a unifying system of communications afforded by a great river and knew the art of writing and keeping records, without which no great civilisation can flourish. Yet they remained a collection of rival city-states, whereas Egypt displayed a national conformity under the leadership of a deity.

For the Pharaoh is a prime example of the god incarnate as king. This concept comes from that stratum in Egyptian culture that belongs to Africa, where similar rulers have existed until recently. A tangible god, whose sole authority could produce results by the exercise of the divine attributes of 'creative utterance', 'understanding' and 'justice', appealed to the Egyptian mentality and gave the nation confidence to overcome formidable obstacles. The Pharaoh from the start was a divine leader whom the entire nation united in following.

The prehistoric rain-maker or pastoral chief who was thought to keep his people, their crops and their cattle, in health and prosperity by exercising a magic control over the weather was thus transformed into the historic Pharaoh, able to sustain and protect the nation by having command over the Nile in a rainless land. Each year he performed ceremonies which were designed to ensure that the waters of the Nile rose with unfailing regularity and were properly used. It was not only the magic throne that he sat on that made the king divine; an ancient folk-yarn relates how the first three kings of the Vth Dynasty were born of the wife of a mere priest by the sun-god, Re himself; and this fiction of a theogamous birth for the Pharaoh is preserved for as long as the kingship lasted in Egypt. The Divine Marriage is represented on several temple walls. The sun-god takes the form of the Pharaoh and fills the Chief Queen with the divine afflatus by holding the sign of life to her nostrils. As a result of this union the heir apparent will be born. Perhaps the most celebrated version of this myth is the one represented on the walls of the funerary temple of Queen Hatshepsut at Western Thebes.

Similarly the coronation of the king, though conducted on earth by chamberlains who had the royal insignia in their charge, was thought to take place in heaven and to be performed by the gods, as is represented on so many temple walls. King Tuthmosis III in the fifteenth century BC claims that it was Amun of Thebes who recognised him as his son as he was serving as a mere boy in the temple at Karnak; and he thereupon flew like a divine falcon to heaven and was crowned by the sun-god: though this is probably a fanciful way of saying that it was his earthly father Tuthmosis II who crowned him in the sanctuary of the temple as his co-regent. The harmony between the divine kingship and the natural world is seen particularly in the intimate connection between the Pharaoh and the Nile on which the prosperity of Egypt depended. Even the sun-worshipping monotheist, Akhenaten, was hailed as 'A Nile which flows daily giving life to Egypt.' The coronation of the king took place at a time which was heralded by the rising of a bright star, Sirius, at the beginning of the inundation. This moment was the auspicious point for the sympathetic rising of a new king and a new Egypt out of the old land drowned in the chaotic waters of the inundation.

Each king, therefore, at his advent was regarded as recreating the old universe anew in the primal pattern that had come down intact from the time when the gods had ruled the earth. Their son and incarnation was on the throne of his ancestors and when he died and was assimilated to Osiris, the god of the dead, his son would reign in his stead. Thus Egypt was eternally under the beneficent rule of God.

Rejoice, O land, in your entirety! A goodly time has come. A Lord has arisen for all countries .... The water stands and fails not and the Nile carries a high flood. The days are long, the nights have hours and the months come aright. The Gods are content and joyful, and life is spent in laughter and wonder.

So sang the scribe at the accession of Mineptah in 1237 BC. 'A Lord has arisen for all countries' – it was not only that the Pharaoh was Lord of Egypt, he was the master of the circuit of the sun's disk. The neighbouring nations recognised that the divine ruler of so rich, so unified and so powerful a state as Egypt was a god indeed. At his advent they journeyed to him bearing rich gifts and seeking his blessing.

The idea of this god incarnate, his birth and coronation, bequeathed a legend and a tradition to the nations of the Near East which persisted for thousands of years.

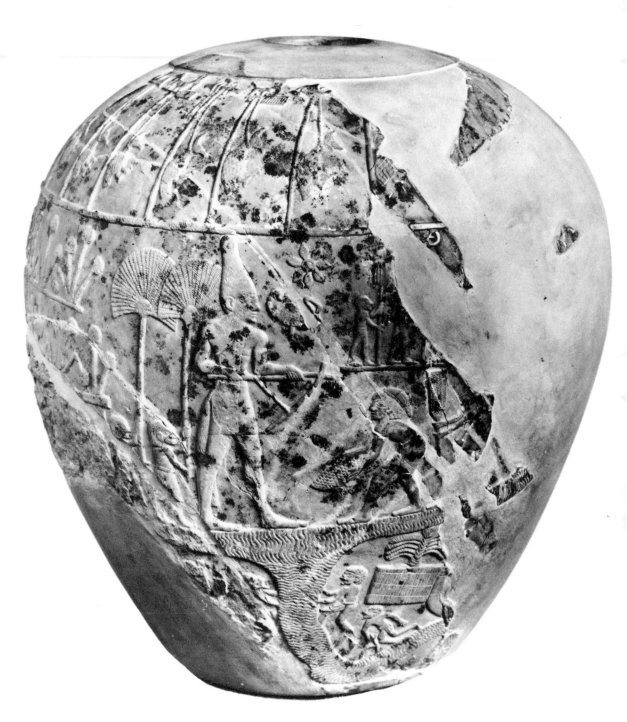

II

Ceremonial macehead of Scorpion, an early ruler, showing him celebrating the rite of 'Opening the Dykes', performed when the inundation began to fall. The king 'cuts the first sod' with a pick while an official waits to remove it in a basket. Beyond the thicket of rushes the Queen waits in her carrying-chair: women dance before her. In the background are standards from which hang plovers and bows signifying Scorpion's sovereignty over Egyptians and foreigners. He wears a tall cap, the White Crown of Upper Egypt, and a tail at his back. In a boat moored nearby he will sail into the new basin he is opening. The prehistoric rainmaker now controls the Nile.

12 (above)
Pyramidion of a fallen granite obelisk at Karnak showing Queen Hatshepsut, who usurped supreme power and is represented as a Pharaoh, kneeling before Amun to have her crown affixed by the god. The crown she wears is the Blue or War Crown, a helmet-like headpiece which makes its appearance in the XVIIth Dynasty. The crowning is performed under the sign for the vault of heaven. The coronation of the King, like his procreation, is the concern only of the gods.

13 (left)
Gilded wood statuette of Tut-ankh-amun as the god Horus of Lower Egypt. He wears the Red Crown and stands upon a papyrus skiff, harpoon in one hand and a chain in the other to capture the animal of Evil who has taken the form of a hippopotamus and hidden in the marshes. Horus, an ancient sky-god, was manifest as a falcon and incarnate in the King. This relationship is expressed in many ways. The King rules – 'while yet in the egg', and on death 'flies to the horizon'. Two of his names bore the title of Horus, and he often wears garments of a feather design.

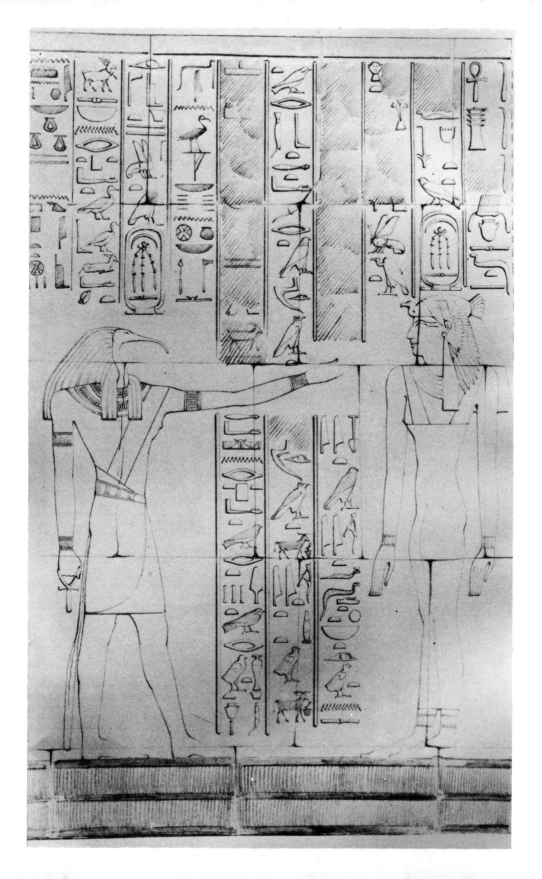

I (above)

Wall-painting from the tomb of Sobek-hotpe showing a delegation of Syrians bringing children and rich gifts to the Pharaoh at his accession. The leaders in their ornate garments fall to the ground and 'smell the earth', before the new god-king upon his throne, in order to beg his blessing. Their gifts consist of gold and silver vessels, an ivory horn full of precious oil, and an eagle-headed rhyton of Mycenaean design probably acquired by trade from the Aegean region. Such scenes also show contingents from Nubia and occasionally from the 'Isles in the Great Green [Mediterranean]'.

14 (left)

The myth of the divine birth, recognition and coronation of the Pharaoh is depicted in several temples. The sun-god takes the form of the Pharaoh and begets the heir-apparent by filling the Chief Queen with the divine afflatus. The drawing opposite shows Thoth, the ibis-headed messenger of the gods, announcing the glad tidings to Queen Ah-mose, the mother of Hatshepsut. Other stages of the myth show the Creator Khnum forming small figures of the 'king' and his soul on a potter's wheel, and the procession to the birth-chamber where the infant is born, recognised by the sun-god and suckled by the divine nurses.

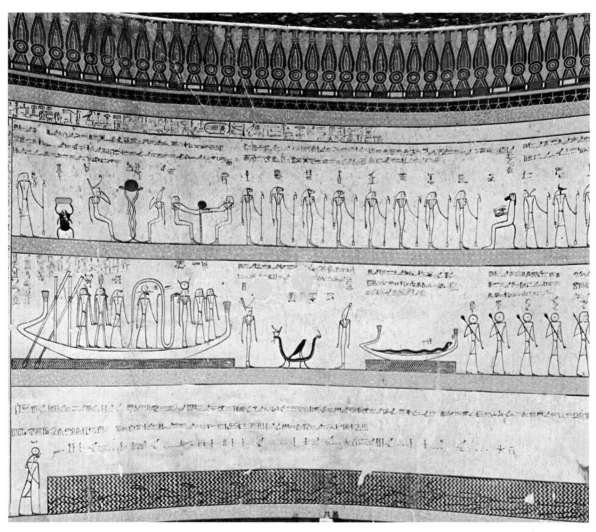

II (above)

The pith of the papyrus sedge which grew abundantly in the marshes of Ancient Egypt could be easily sliced into strips which, when laid edge to edge and crossed with similar strips at right angles, only needed a light pressing to dry into sheets of paper. Such sheets could be pasted together to form rolls. New papyrus was white and pliable but as it aged it became yellow and brittle. The walls of the burial chamber of King Tuthmosis III are decorated as though an ancient copy of 'The Book of What is in the Underworld' has been unrolled against them, and the ground is painted yellow to show its antiquity.

III (right)

At the redness of sunset, Re stepped from the day-boat into the night-boat. The sun-god, now in the form of a ram-headed being called Flesh, bears the sun-disk on his head and is protected by the coils of a huge serpent. He is accompanied by divinities in the boat as it is towed on the waters under the earth through the regions of the night hours, illuminating the Underworld, overcoming its hostile denizens and undergoing transformations which will result in his being born at the next dawn as Kheperer, the scarab, a name which means 'coming into existence'. This painted relief of the night-boat with its crew is in the tomb of Sethos I. Below, the sun-god Atum overcomes the serpent fiend Apophis.

IV

Scene on the side of a painted box, showing Tut-ankh-amun vanquishing Asiatics who fall headlong before his strong right arm. He is mounted in a chariot, shooting into a disordered mass of the enemy distinguishable by their heavy beards, long-sleeved garments and rectangular bucklers. The king is accompanied by his mounted suite and two negro fan-bearers. The scene is more fantastic than real. The ordered calm of the Pharaoh, the embodiment of right, contrasts with the confused mass of the enemy, symbols of error and evil.

V

'A goodly burial' was the ideal to which every Egyptian who was rich enough aspired. 'Remember the day of burial, the passing into bliss when the night shall be consecrated to you with oils and bandages. A procession is formed . . . your coffin is gilded, its head inlaid with lapis lazuli, a canopy above it. You are placed on the bier and oxen draw you. Then the musicians shall await your coming and the mourners dance before the door of your tomb.' Part of the funeral procession of the Vizier Ramose, showing professional mourners beating their breasts and pouring dust on their heads while servants carry objects he used in life for deposition in his 'mansion of eternity'.

VI (above)

A scene painted on a wall in the tomb of the King's land agent, Menna, showing scribes with cords knotted at standard lengths measuring the standing crops to estimate the yield. On the right a farmer and his small son conduct the scribes through the fields while another tenant and his wife bring them a corn-dolly and first-fruits. Below, scribes with their writing palettes and document cases record the yield of winnowed grain as it is measured out in standard containers. From such records, a document like the Wilbour Papyrus (plate 38) would be compiled.

VII (right)

At his advent Tut-ankh-amun claimed that Egypt was 'topsy-turvy' through the religious revolution of his predecessor Akhenaten, who had banished the old gods in favour of his sole deity, the Aten. Tut-ankh-amun had to restore the nation's morale and prosperity by returning to the former way of life and the worship of the old gods. Their neglected shrines were rebuilt, their estates re-endowed and their destroyed images remade. This statue at Karnak shows Amun, the god of Thebes who had suffered most under Akhenaten, carved in the reign of Tut-ankh-amun with his features.

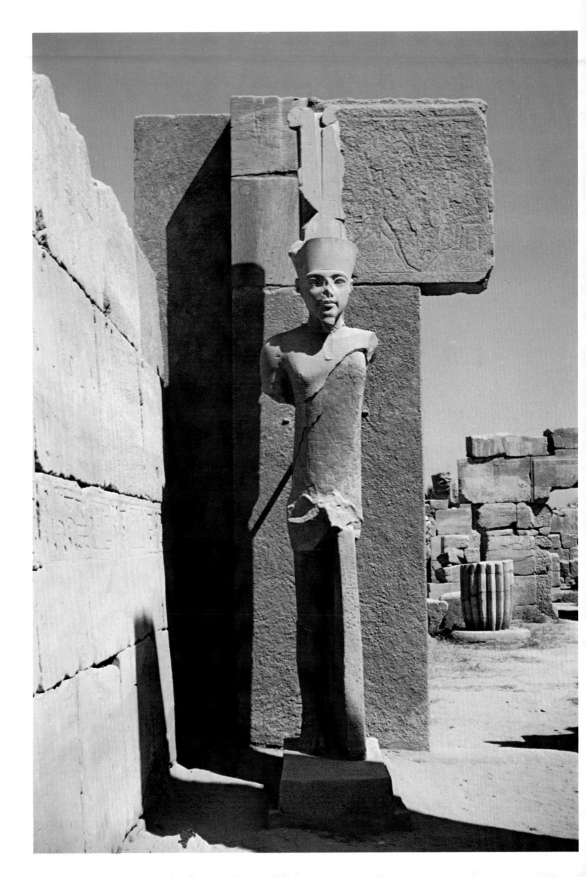

VIII (above)

The cycle of the reincarnation of the god who ruled Egypt at each new reign is seen in the features of the Osiris myth where his son, Horus, took his place on the throne of the living, while the murdered god was resurrected to rule the realm of the dead. Each new Horus, who was usually the son of his predecessor, in turn was assimilated to Osiris on death (plate 78). In this wall-painting from the tomb of Tut-ankh-amun, the successor, Ay, in the dress of a living king, performs the last rites for his predecessor who is shown as the mummified Osiris, even though Ay was much older than Tut-ankh-amun and not his son.

15 (right)

Carved and painted wooden head of the infant Tut-ankh-amun emerging from a lotus flower. According to a myth popular at Hermopolis, creation began when out of the ocean of Chaos a lotus arose and opened its petals to disclose the young sun-god whose light dispelled the darkness on the face of the waters. The advent of the new Pharaoh is often represented as the appearance of a child upon a lotus, since he was the son of the sun-god and each king was believed to re-create the Egyptian universe in the old form at the beginning of his reign.

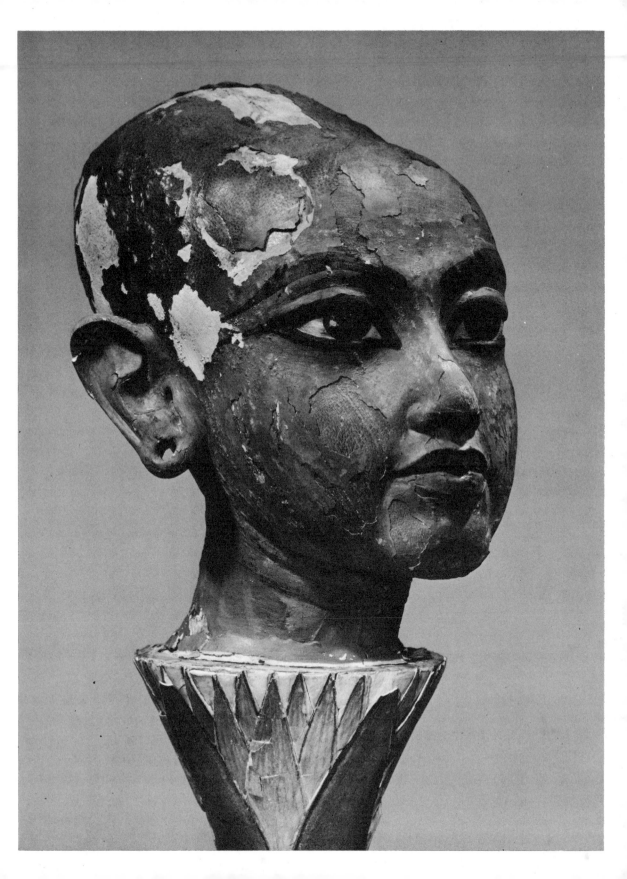

16
Relief from his temple at Abydos showing Sethos I, c. 1317 BC, wearing the *Atefu* Crown, with horns, feathers and sun-disks of his coronation. He holds the crook and 'flail' and has a false beard attached to his chin – all reminders of the prehistoric origin of the Pharaoh as a pastoral chieftain. He sits on a throne personified by the mother goddess, Isis, who thus 'makes the King', an idea common in Africa where chiefs' stools play a similar role. Sethos is supported by the goddesses of Upper and Lower Egypt, here represented as elegant queens. The gods Horus and Thoth bind the symbolic plants of Upper and Lower Egypt beneath him.

3　The Pharaoh as Hero

The horse-drawn chariot, introduced into the Eastern Mediterranean about the eighteenth century BC during the latest phases of the Bronze Age, wrought a greater revolution in the world of the time than the motor-car has effected in our own day. It was not only that a new and formidable armoured vehicle was introduced into the warfare of the period, but great changes were precipitated in the entire social system of the Ancient World. The warrior society that is mirrored in *The Iliad*, with its aristocracy of armoured chariot fighters, expert in the use of the javelin and the composite bow, and with its emphasis upon athletic contests and the management of horses, spread all over the Near East forming a professional military caste who established feudal states in Syria and Palestine among the petty rulers.

The Pharaohs of the New Kingdom, who were the Egyptian contemporaries of this last period of the Bronze Age, did not escape these novel ideas. Instead of the remote divine king of former ages, more of a god than a priest, and more of a priest than a warrior, the Pharaoh himself now took the field in person at the head of professional armies, the incarnation of a war-god like Baal, or Mont. To the traditional garb of a prehistoric divine king the Pharaohs added a new crown, the Blue Crown or war helmet, and replaced the old mace by a modern scimitar which even became a sceptre like the pastoral 'crook' and so-called 'flail'. Like the heroes of *The Iliad* they boasted of the harness that they had stripped off their vanquished foes. Above all, they delighted to show themselves as vainglorious Homeric champions mounted in a chariot and charging into the thick of the foe or herds of wild animals; while their prowess as athletes, archers or sportsmen is vaunted as truly superhuman. In particular Amenophis II, in a stela found near the Great Sphinx at Giza, is fulsomely praised for his sporting and military exploits. Such a divine hero had to have a memorial that not only sustained his mortuary cult but left some record of his great deeds to posterity.

It was at Thebes, the birth-place of their dynasty, that these champions chose to have their last resting-place dedicated to their own cults and that of the hero-god of Thebes, Amun. For this purpose they selected a remote and wild gorge on the western bank of Thebes, now known as the Valley of the Kings, where their tombs were hewn, some of them, like that of Sethos I, vast complexes of halls and corridors, decorated with extracts from the sacred books; but some, like that of Tut-ankh-amun, a few modest chambers, mostly bare. Only the tomb of Tut-ankh-amun has been found substantially intact. The last resting-places of nearly thirty of his fellow rulers had been plundered by the end of the New Kingdom and their occupants stripped of their opulent trappings. The royal tomb with its treasure and its occupants was in a secret place. The public part of the memorial was the mortuary temple built in a row of such structures in the plain that flanked the west bank of the Nile at Thebes, separated from the Valley of Kings by a ridge of hills.

Most of these temples are little more than heaps of rubble or mere ground-plans under the sand, but the ruins of one or two others are more impressive, such as the mortuary temple of Queen Hatshepsut dominating the amphi-theatre at Deir el-Bahri, and the temple of Ramesses II, known today as the Ramesseum. The most complete, however, is the mortuary temple of Ramesses III at Medinet Habu. Ramesses III, the last great native Pharaoh of Egypt, in the twelfth century BC had the task of beating back from the borders of Egypt invasions of land-hungry Libyans and assaults by con-federations of migrants known as the 'Sea Peoples', whose incursions into Asia Minor, the islands of the Aegean and the North African coast destroyed the old cultures of the Late Bronze Age in the Eastern Mediterranean, a mere decade after the fall of Troy VII. These great deeds are depicted on the walls of the mortuary temple at Medinet Habu, the defeat of the two waves of Libyans being dated to years five and eleven, and the repulse of the Sea Peoples to year eight. The latter, among whom appear forerunners of the Philistines, Dardanians, Lycians, Sicilians and other peoples of the Classical World, are shown in their peculiar ships in a great naval battle off the Nile mouths, the first representation of such warfare in history.

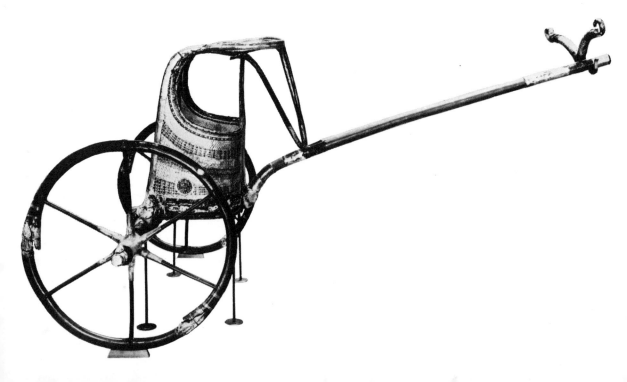

17 and 18

The horse-drawn chariots of Ancient Egypt are masterpieces of wood-working, many different species of woods being selected for the particular part they had to play in the construction. It is certain that their invention and development arose elsewhere, though there are representations of chariots being made in Egypt. They were frequently sent as gifts to the Pharaoh by the rulers of Asia. The bodies of the great state chariots were ornamented with reliefs, gilded and inlaid with coloured glass and glazes, so that when the king appeared in them it was likened to the sun-god arising in his glory. Above, is a detail of the decoration of the chariot. The bodies of these vehicles were made of wood coated with gesso, modelled in relief and covered with gold foil. The scene shows a Northern foe, an Amorite, between two Southern enemies, both negroes. All the foreigners are represented pinioned and kneeling in supplication, bound by cords in the form of the plant of Lower Egypt.

19 (above)

Part of the reliefs in the mortuary temple of Queen Hatshepsut (plate 24) showing the reception of an Egyptian trading mission by Pairohu, the Chief of Punt, a mysterious land in East Africa reached by vessels from a Red Sea port. Nehesi, the Egyptian commander, accompanied by a bodyguard, offers in exchange for myrrh, myrrh-trees, gold, ivory and other tropical products, the traditional goods of all such traders to Africa – beads and weapons. Other scenes in the same reliefs show the loading of the boats, the journey to Thebes, the unloading of the cargo and its dedication to Amun of Thebes. The scene illustrates one of the great 'deeds' that the Queen accomplished during her reign.

20 (left)

A granite stela found at Karnak showing King Amenophis II, like a Homeric champion in his chariot, shooting arrows through an ingot of bronze and a wooden target. A stela found near Memphis says of him, 'He drew 300 strong bows comparing the skill of the different bowyers ... And afterwards he mounted a chariot like the war-god Mont in his might and shot his arrows in turn at four targets of copper each a palm thick mounted on posts .... It was a fabulous deed to shoot at such targets so that his arrows went right through them and dropped to the ground.'

21 (above)
The third King of the XVIIIth Dynasty began the tradition of having the tomb of the Pharaoh hewn in a barren wady at Western Thebes, the birthplace of his family. In this spot, now known as the Valley of the Kings, were buried thirty Pharaohs who ruled from 1510 to 1085 BC. Their tombs were robbed in antiquity and their stripped mummies hidden in two caches not discovered until the last century. Although the tomb of Tut-ankh-amun had also been violated, it is the only one to have remained substantially intact. The view in the foreground shows the entrances to the tombs of Sethos I and Ramesses I.

22 (right above)
Some of the tombs have been discovered only during the past seventy years. Others have stood open since classical times and still bear the scribbles of Greek visitors, such as the tomb of Ramesses VI (c. 1150 BC), a hall of which is illustrated here. This chamber is elaborately decorated with scenes from the Book of Gates and the Book of Caverns. The four pillars show the King making offerings to the gods of Thebes.

23 (right below)
Ramesses II at his accession receives sceptres handed to him by Amun, seated upon a throne and supported by his consort, Mut, shown as an elegant woman wearing the vulture headdress of a queen-mother and the united crowns of Upper and Lower Egypt. The emblems of rule consist of the traditional pastoral crook and flail and also the new curved scimitar that was introduced from Asia in the eighteenth century BC with other chariot weapons such as the composite bow and the war helmet, a version of which, the Blue Crown, is here worn by Ramesses II.

24 (above)
The mortuary temple to sustain the cult of the dead King was built about a mile away from the tomb in the western plain at Thebes. One of the earliest to survive, though in a greatly ruined state, is this temple of Queen Hatshepsut at Deir el-Bahri, built on three terraces. The walls of the colonnades are decorated with scenes showing the Queen's great deeds, such as the erection of obelisks (plate 64) and the trading expedition sent to the spice-lands of Punt (plate 19). It also depicts the Queen's divine conception, birth and recognition (plate 14).

25 (right above)
The mortuary temple of Ramesses III is the most complete of such edifices. It was surrounded by a stout wall pierced by two fortified gates. Here the entire population of Western Thebes took sanctuary in the later years of the XXth Dynasty when marauding bands of Libyans were roving at large. In the foreground is a palace adjoining the First Court where the King and his suite stayed during his visits to Thebes. On the exterior North wall, reliefs show the King attacking foreign foes including the ship-borne Sea Peoples who overran Asia during his reign.

26 (right below)
The Ramesseum is the modern name for the mortuary temple of Ramesses II which stands in picturesque ruin on the edge of the cultivation at Thebes. Its Egyptian name was The House of Usimaré (i.e. Ozymandias, Ramesses II) in the Estate of Amun. Its pylons, courts and halls are considerably dilapidated but scenes of the King's exploits still remain on some of the walls (plate 49); chiefly his wars in Syria against the Hittites and their vassals. The First Court had a colossal seated statue of the King nearly 60 feet high hewn from a single block of granite and weighing over a thousand tons which now lies shattered (far right), and inspired the sonnet *Ozymandias* by Shelley.

27

The great deeds of Ramesses III are depicted on the outer walls of his temple (plate 25) where he drives evil, in the form of the enemies of Egypt and the animals of the wild, from the holy precincts. Here, with his sons acting as beaters, he rounds up wild cattle in the papyrus thickets by the banks of a stream. Above, still in a chariot, he hunts the animals of the desert.

4 Officials of the King

It was the officials of the Palace, a sort of Privy Council, who helped the king to govern and who in the tomb of Tut-ankh-amun are represented in a unique scene showing them wearing their white mourning bands, faithful to the end, hauling the catafalque of their dead lord on his last journey to the West.

This scene belongs more to private tombs and a splendid example may be seen in that of the Vizier Ramose. These are also the high officers of state at the time of Tut-ankh-amun, and the Egyptian equivalent of the military aristocracy that had spread with their chariots all over the Near East. Such intimates of the king might be related to him by marriage, but some claim to have been men of lowly origin who had distinguished themselves by valour in the field. Others had been brought up with the king, their mothers having been wet-nurses of the royal children. Such families tended to form dynasties of officials, their sons or nephews succeeding them in turn.

The chief offices were those of the two Overseers of the Treasury, concerned with the reception and allocation of raw materials and finished goods, plunder, tribute, and other commodities. Also important was the Overseer of the Granaries of Upper and Lower Egypt whose responsibility was the harvesting, recording and storage of the annual crops of wheat and barley. There were many other court posts such as the Chief Steward, the Master of the Horse, the Scribe of the Recruits, the First Herald, Secretary and Butler besides various underlings, chamberlains, pages and fanbearers – though the title of 'fanbearer on the right of the king' was claimed as an honorary position by the highest officers in the land.

Two officials during the New Kingdom were of especial importance. The first, a new post, was the Viceroy of Kush, the king's deputy in Nubia and the Sudan as far as the 4th Cataract. His seat of government was at Aniba, 140 miles south of the 1st Cataract, and from here he ruled his provinces in the names of the Pharaoh with an administration modelled on that of Egypt itself.

The other official was the First Prophet, or High Priest of Amun at Thebes, whose temple received such enormous endowments and gifts from grateful Pharaohs that the person who administered its considerable wealth could not fail to become an important power in the state.

The chief official under the king during the New Kingdom, however, was still the vizier whose office goes back to the dawn of history and persisted until the fourth century BC. Generally at this period there were two viziers serving in Upper and Lower Egypt. One of them, Rekh-mi-re, who served Tuthmosis III, has left in his tomb a detailed account of his duties. These included not only a daily report to his sovereign on the state of the nation but also the delivering of judgements in his Audience Hall, the receiving and issuing of instructions to the various branches of central government, and the making and rescinding of appointments.

He was chiefly concerned with the collection of taxes in Upper and Lower Egypt, but he also mobilised the king's personal bodyguard; saw to the cutting of timber and general irrigation; directed village headmen as to summer cultivation; made a weekly inspection of the water resources; considered deficits in temple revenues and assessments for taxation. He also confirmed the state of the fortresses on the borders; took measures against raids by robbers and nomads, and saw to the fitting out of ships. He presided over important civil cases referred to him from lower courts; he dealt with questions of land tenure and the witnessing of wills; and he considered criminal cases requiring heavy sentences, all in his capacity of Chief Justice. He also received foreign embassies, and supervised workshops and building enterprises including the work on the Royal Tomb. No wonder that the Pharaoh, in delivering the homily that it was customary to address to high officials when they took office, should say to Rekh-mi-re:

Look to the office of the vizier. Be vigilant about what is done in it, for it is the mainstay of the entire land. As to the vizierate, it is not sweet, indeed, but it is bitter as gall. For the vizier is hard copper enclosing the gold of his master's house.

The king went on to warn the new incumbent against using his rank to further his own interest. He is to show favour to no one.

These then were the king's high officials and some of the principles by which they were supposed to govern. Such officials were well recompensed because, as an early Pharaoh remarked to his son, a poorly paid official is open to corruption. Such men formed the administrative arm of government.

28

High officials of Tut-ankh-amun wearing white mourning bands around their heads and drawing the catafalque of their dead lord to his tomb. They comprise the privy council that helped the King to govern. In the penultimate row are the two viziers of Upper and Lower Egypt with their shaven heads and long gowns. The last man in the cortège must be the King's Deputy for the Army. Probably also included, though not identified, are the Viceroy of Nubia and Kush, the King's First and Second Heralds, the Overseers of the Treasury, the Chief Steward, the High Priests of Amun, the Elders of Thebes and the Overseer of Works.

29 (above)

King Amenophis II as a child on the lap of his wet-nurse, Amen-em-ipet. He is shown as a miniature Pharaoh complete with regalia, his feet resting on a footstool decorated with the bound figures of the traditional nine nations whom he leads captive with cords. Ken-amun, a son of Amen-em-ipet and therefore the King's foster-brother and companion from earliest days, was appointed his High Steward upon his accession to the throne. Such families of officials tended to follow one another in office, the son succeeding the father for several generations.

30 (right)

The audience chamber of the Vizier Rekh-mi-re, in his capacity as Chief Justice, showing its windows and the tall columns that support the roof. Lesser magistrates are drawn up in two lines to the left and right with their scribes holding writing palettes. In the central aisle, and outside the hall, ushers are introducing the litigants or debtors. Two messengers arrive at the double with dispatches and are met by janitors. The vizier is said to be 'holding a session to hear [law suits] in the hall . . . dispensing justice impartially . . . no petitioner weeping because of him.'

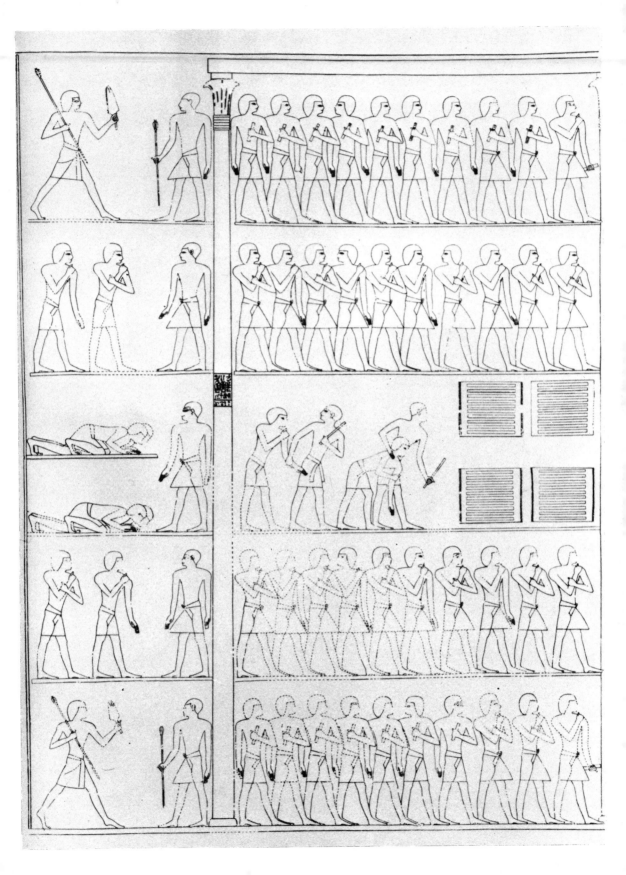

31 (above)

Huy, the Viceroy of Kush, who governed Nubia and the Lower Sudan in the name of the King during the reign of Tut-ankh-amun. He is shown on the right carrying two formal bouquets as he leaves the palace after his appointment, and is accompanied by his sons who also carry flowers. One of them succeeded him as Viceroy. On the left, in the upper register, holding his fan of office, Huy receives his commission from a Chief Treasurer who says, 'Thus decrees Pharaoh – "there is handed over to you from El Kab to Napata"' (the extent of the province he is to govern). In the lower scenes Huy receives a gold signet ring, his seal of office.

32 (far left)

A black granite statue, now in Turin, of the Second Prophet of Amun, Anen, wearing the leopard skin of his office. The princes of Thebes, who drove the Asiatic Hyksos kings off the throne of Egypt in the sixteenth century BC, gave large endowments to Amun, the god of their native city who had promoted their fortunes. This great wealth was administered by four prophets or High Priests who became very influential in state affairs. Anen, who held office for much of the reign of Amenophis III, was the brother-in-law of the king and the uncle of Tut-ankh-amun.

33 (left)

Black granite statue, in Cairo, of the Vizier Woser and his wife, showing him wearing the distinctive gown upheld by a halter. Woser was preceded in office by his father, and succeeded by his nephew, during the long reign of Tuthmosis III. All these officials left detailed accounts in their tombs of their duties and appointments. Every morning, explains one, the Vizier 'is to enter the Great Palace, and as soon as he appears at the portal the Chief Treasurer is to advance and meet him saying, "All your affairs are safe and sound, and the Royal Estate is safe and sound."'

34

The Southern Vizier was also responsible for the collection of taxes in Upper Egypt from the First Cataract almost to Amarna in Middle Egypt. Here the headmen of Elephantine bring their taxes in kind, to be recorded and checked by the officials. In the top register, chests of cloth, gold and silver beads and gold rings are received. In the central register the gold is weighed. In the bottom register a policeman escorts a tax-payer who presents cloths, bundles of sticks, cordage, baskets of fruit and ten grindstones. In addition, cattle, honey, pigeons, grain, beans, gum and grass mats were delivered.

5   Scribes

In a land so dependent upon the control of the flood waters for its prosperity, the Egyptians had been accustomed from earliest times to an organised way of life, but their highly centralised administration would not have been possible without the discovery of writing and it is probable that the development of the machinery of state and the art of writing went hand in hand.

The character that writing took in Egypt was due to the invention of a remarkable material – papyrus – one of the great contributions of the Egyptians to civilisation. As early as the fourth millennium BC, the Egyptians had learnt to make a flexible paper from the pith of the papyrus sedge which grew in profusion in the undrained verges of cultivation.

The Egyptian practice of writing in ink on this paper, and very occasionally on leather, was already in force at the very dawn of history; but all the evidence is that the art of writing was used not so much to create works of literature as to preserve records and documents of a profusion and complexity that can only be paralleled in modern times with the widespread use of a paper made from rags.

The extreme compactness and portability of Egyptian documents made it possible to develop filing systems and to keep repositories of records for hundreds of years. There are several references to the consulting of ancient archives in temple libraries and sometimes of papyri so old that gaps had been worn or eaten into the texts. No other nation of antiquity had such convenient means for retaining a memory of its past and documenting every aspect of its life and activities.

Despite the wealth of papyri that exists in the storerooms of most great collections, the mass that has survived is an infinitesimal proportion of what was written in antiquity. The paper-work by which the Egyptian machinery of state functioned was obviously very voluminous and highly organised, but it is clear that it could never have operated without the existence of an educated and busy legion of scribes, able to read, write and calculate and keep such records. This class formed a bureaucratic élite versed in the art of writing and aware of its privileges. 'The scribe,' wrote one of their number in a composition that was popular with schoolboys a century after the death of Tut-ankh-amun, 'directs the work of everyone. For him there are no taxes, he pays his dues in writing.' 'It is the scribe,' wrote another, 'who assesses and collects the taxes in Upper and Lower Egypt. He governs the entire country and every affair is under his control.'

The training of a scribe began at a very early age and was completed by the time he reached manhood at about sixteen. The pupil was sent to one of the schools attached to the great departments of state such as the Palace, the Treasury and the Army, or to the 'Houses of Life', the scriptoria attached to the larger temples where books and inscriptions were copied and compiled. The wealth of school exercises that has survived shows that most scribes had to spend part of their time instructing pupils, probably their sons or relations, since education in Egypt was largely on the master and apprentice system.

In learning the classical utterance of the Middle Kingdom which was used for some monumental and religious purposes down to Roman times, the pupil often had to contend with a language which was already dead and which he understood only imperfectly as his copies of the classics clearly reveal. But it is often only in this garbled form that Egyptian literature has come down to us. When the young scribe had graduated from school he had his foot upon the first rung of a career in the higher ranks of the Army, the Treasury or the Palace. While a career open to all the talents was hardly possible in Ancient Egypt, where the tradition was to appoint the son to the place of his father from the Pharaoh down to the merest field labourer, it did sometimes happen that a man from humble circumstances attained to high office. In the exhortation to be a scribe which the master set his pupil to copy, the rewards of successful graduation are enticingly set forth.

A man of worth is sought for, and you are found. The man that is skilled rises step by step until he has attained the position of a magistrate.

It was through his command of writing in the hieratic and hieroglyphic scripts that the scribe for so long made Ancient Egypt the most highly organised and prosperous state in the Near East. We have in this chapter been concerned only with the scribe as a civil servant; but in addition to his accounts, reports, legal texts, letters and government files, he also produced a wide literature – novels, poems, lyrics, hymns, meditations, instructions and lamentations, as well as mathematical, surgical and medical treatises. That these were not the least esteemed of their writings is clear from a eulogy on the ancient authors written by a scribe in the thirteenth century BC.

Their monuments have crumbled in pieces. Their mortuary priests have gone; their tomb-stones are covered with sand; their chambers forgotten. But their names are pronounced because of the good books that they wrote and their memory is for ever more.

---

35 (right)
Part of the writing equipment of Tut-ankh-amun comprising an ivory palette with reed pens and two ink-pans, and a pen-case in the form of a palm-column made of wood overlaid with gold and inlaid with coloured glass. The writing palettes of several members of the royal family at this period, men and women, have survived as reminders that the Ancient Egyptian Pharaohs and their children, unlike medieval European Kings, were able to read and write. Earlier, the Pyramid Texts of the Old Kingdom had spoken of the Pharaoh as acting as the scribe of the sun-god after death.

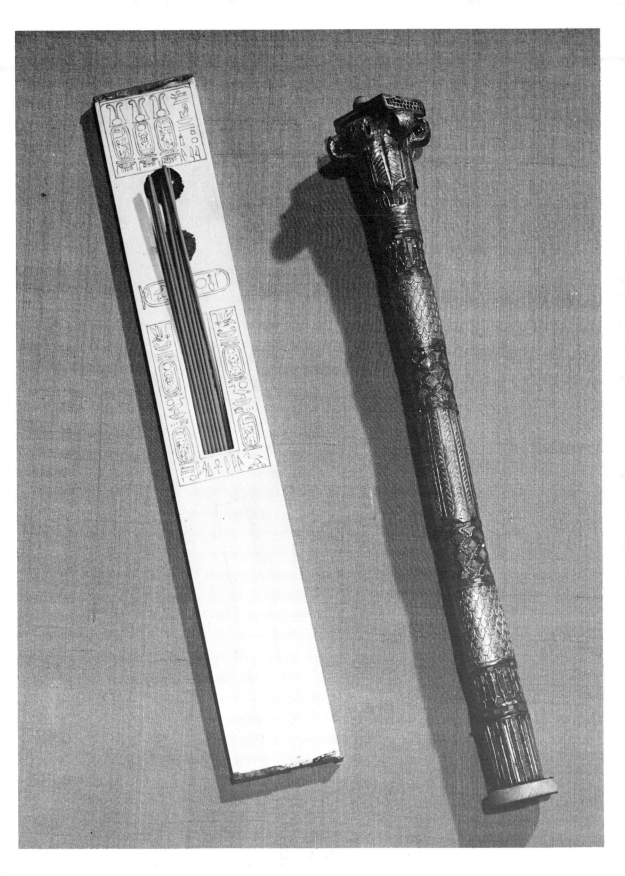

36 (above)
While Egyptian society tended to be fixed in rigid patterns, in which the son followed the calling of his father, it did sometimes happen that a man from humble circumstances attained to high office, particularly if he had been taught reading and writing. A notable case is Sennemut, the Chief Steward and general factotum of Queen Hatshepsut, whose father bore only a vague and probably posthumous title of 'worthy'. He rose by merit to high office under the Queen and was given the honorary position of tutor to her daughter Neferu-re whom he is seen nursing in this statue in Cairo.

37 (right)
Egyptian hieroglyphs are the most beautiful forms of writing ever devised, and it is probable that their aesthetic qualities as well as their hallowed tradition kept them in use for so long, especially for monumental inscriptions. At the end of their life in the Ptolemaic and Roman periods when they were employed as an esoteric mystery, they display remarkably ugly forms and a confused 'typography'. In the high periods of Egyptian culture, however, they reveal the same elegant proportions and drawing as the contemporary reliefs. In this panel two of the titles and names of King Sesostris I of the XIIth Dynasty, protected by the flying falcon Horus of Edfu, are spaced out in elegant glyphs carved in great detail.

38 (left)
The Wilbour Papyrus in the Brooklyn Museum, shown here before it was unrolled, is a fiscal survey of the various plots of cultivated land in a continuous portion of Middle Egypt, from near modern Minia to a point some eighty miles north, made in about a month during summer in the fourth regnal year of Ramesses V (c. 1156 BC). This register gives in meticulous detail particulars of the different institutions that owned the various tracts of land, the names of the farmers, the estimated yields and their assessments for taxation. Such a chance survival enables us to estimate the enormous mass of paperwork by which the Egyptian State functioned.

39 (above)
Hieroglyphs were used only for monumental and religious purposes. A more cursive and abbreviated way of writing them, called today hieratic, soon developed. In hieratic the resemblance to the original picture sign is often vestigial, and the system underwent its own evolution in spelling and grammar. The above part of a pupil's exercise is written in hieratic of the period of about a century after Tut-ankh-amun. Schoolboys were set to copy the classics, in this case, two model letters, and often their garbled versions are the only copies now existing. The master has corrected the exercise by writing more correct versions of some words and dating the exercise in the upper margin.

40

Ostrakon, or flake of limestone, written in hieratic script, a cursive development of hieroglyphs, with part of a poem on the king in his panoply of war. Papyrus was too precious to be used for school exercises and potsherds or flakes of limestone were used instead. This ostrakon, written on both sides, is at Edinburgh and is continued on another ostrakon in Turin. It describes the royal war-chariot and abounds in Canaanite words and different puns on them. Since the chariot was an Asiatic import, however, the pupil would have learnt the foreign terms for the various parts by memorising this poem.

41
Serpentine statuette of a scribe reading under the inspiration of Thoth, the god of wisdom and learning. The scribe squats tailor-wise, his gown drawn tight across his thighs to form a table for his papyrus roll which is open at one end. On an altar squats the god, here in the form of one of his familiars, the baboon, who should bear on his head the crescent and disk of the moon which are his symbols as the reckoner of time, since the Egyptian calendar was primarily lunar.

6 Soldiers of the Pharaoh

The Egypt of Tut-ankh-amun had come to know the soldier as an important and permanent element in the society of the day, and the influential advisers of the king were nearly all high ranking officers of the chariotry and the infantry, though in earlier times the army had played a much more self-effacing role.

It was, however, in the New Kingdom, after the introduction of the horse-drawn chariot by the Asiatic Hyksos kings, that warfare became mobile again and the fortress, so characteristic of the strategy of the Feudal Age and the Middle Kingdom, became as much a depot as a bastion. With the chariot came new arms and armour, new methods of warfare and a military aristocracy, as we have mentioned earlier. The small standing army of the Old and Middle Kingdoms was expanded into a large professional organisation with squadrons of chariots, each manned by a driver and fighter, and armed with such new weapons as the composite bow, heavy bronze falchion and battle-axe. Military standards enabled units to be readily located on the field of battle and instructions could be signalled by means of the war-trumpet. Engagements became more than the shock of armed bodies meeting in a general mêlée. Strategy and tactics became the concern of the Pharaohs and their war-councils; and if we are to believe the official accounts it was, for instance, the plan of battle devised by Tuthmosis III that was responsible for his great victory at Megiddo over a confederation of Asiatic princes, though the indiscipline of his raw troops lost him the early fruits of victory.

The Egyptian forces, under the supreme command of the Pharaoh or his deputy, were divided into four armies named after the principal gods. There was an elaborate chain of field command from the generals and battalion commanders through the standard-bearers to the platoon leaders. In addition, staff duties were performed by a multitude of military scribes who attended to the commissariat and other logistical matters. Thus Haremhab, the Commander-in-Chief under Tut-ankh-amun, whose footsteps on the battlefield he claimed to have guided, chose to have himself represented as a scribe reading a hymn to the god of writing in a granite statue now in New York. Haremhab subsequently became king on the death of Tut-ankh-amun's successor, Ay, another soldier who before his elevation to the throne had been in charge of the chariotry.

The reputations of such men lay in their ability to dispose of a great mass of manpower, for one of the main tasks of the army in time of peace was to act as a labour force for the quarrying of stone, the working of the gold and turquoise mines and the erection of great monuments.

In the earlier part of the XVIIIth Dynasty, the armies were manned by native Egyptians and Nubian auxiliaries who followed the family calling. But the pick of the young men called up for service in the general corvée were also conscripted particularly for the labour force. From the reign of Amenophis III, however, it became the practice to draft foreign captives into the Egyptian forces. After the end of our period the Egyptian armies were manned more and more by foreigners – Libyans, Sudanis and finally Carian and Greek mercenaries. The Wilbour papyrus lists a number of cultivators in Middle Egypt who bear foreign names and were evidently veteran soldiers settled on the land.

Despite what the satirist had to say about the miserable life of the soldier, its rewards were considerable. Warriors who had shown bravery in the field were promoted to officers, given prisoners as serfs and decorated with 'the gold of valour'. Such awards took the form of massive flies in gold, gold or silver weapons and jewellery of considerable intrinsic value.

Even the less distinguished soldier shared in the cattle, weapons, clothing, ornaments and other loot captured from luxurious Asiatic enemies. He was pensioned off with grants of livestock, serfs, and land, from the royal domains, on which he paid taxes but which continued to be held by his family as long as they had an able-bodied male available for military service. Such soldiers formed a privileged class, devoted to the tradition of service in the armed forces. In times of peace they dwelt in comfortable settlements.

Experienced military scribes and officers were appointed to positions in the foreign service as ambassadors or district commissioners, and to such court posts as stewards of the royal estates, butlers, fan-bearers, police-chiefs and instructors to the young princes or even major-domos to the king's daughters. Whenever the hereditary succession to the throne died out at the end of a dynasty, it was these warrior intimates of the king who stepped into his empty sandals.

---

42 (right)
Another detail from the painted box of Tut-ankh-amun (plate IV) showing Egyptian foot soldiers moving over the battlefield cutting off the hands of slain negroes for the final count of victory. The infantry, in contrast to the immaculate sun-king and his mounted escort, are painted with marked realism showing them with several days' growth of beard and unkempt hair, their cut-leather aprons and garments tarnished with the stains of battle, as though the artist had remembered the words of the satirist in recounting the lot of the infantryman – 'he is born only to be torn from the arms of his mother. He is battered and bruised with floggings.'

43
A relief, now in Bologna, showing scenes of military life. On the right a squad of soldiers is labouring under a great baulk of timber, while a mounted scout dashes into the camp. 'The infantryman marches to Syria,' continues the satirist, 'his bread and water borne on his back like the load of an ass.' But the aristocratic charioteer fared no better – 'When he has acquired a goodly span he is overjoyed and tears madly around his home town with them, but he does not know what is in store for him . . . . When he reaches the mountains he has to cast his expensive chariot into a thicket and go on foot . . . . When he reports back he is beaten with a hundred blows.'

44

Egyptian chariotry waiting to go into action against the Hittites, from the reliefs on the exterior walls of the temple of Ramesses II at Abydos. The Egyptian chariots were manned by two warriors, a groom and a fighter carrying a large round-topped shield. His weapons were the composite bow and a light javelin hurled with the aid of a spear-thrower. (These are carried in cases strapped to the side of the car.) The Hittite chariots held three men (plate 49). If we are to believe the same satirist again, the chariot officer got his position because he came of good family, 'he squanders his patrimony on an expensive chariot in which he drives furiously.'

45
Black granite statue of Amenophis-son-of-Hapu, the great minister of Amenophis III, who was noted for his wisdom and learning and later deified. He is shown in his capacity of a military scribe, i.e. a staff officer, the Scribe of the Recruits. In this capacity he was responsible for organising all the training, supply and manpower of the armed forces. The army was also used on great public works, such as the hewing, transport and erection of the so-called Colossi of Memnon in front of the now-vanished mortuary temple of Amenophis III at Western Thebes.

46

A relief, now at Leyden, showing another high-ranking military scribe, the General Haremhab, who claimed to have guided the footsteps of his King on the battlefields of Asia, being decorated with the Award of Gold at the accession of Tut-ankh-amun. He is in festal garb with a cone of perfumed unguent on his head. He raises his arms in the sign of jubilation as chamberlains hang the gold collars around his neck. It was such experienced soldiers who in the military state of Egypt during the New Kingdom were best able to ascend the throne when the royal line died out.

47
The Egyptian armies gradually came to be manned by foreign mercenaries, some of whom were defeated enemies who took service with their captors. Akhenaten had a bodyguard of Libyan, Asiatic and negro soldiers. This stela, also of his reign, shows a Syrian spearman with his wife, being waited upon by an Egyptian servant who helps him to drink wine through a reed syphon. This anticipates the boast of Ramesses III that, through his pacification, 'The bows and weapons [of the mercenaries] reposed in the armouries. Their wives and children were beside them as they ate and drank at ease.' Such soldiers were settled on the land and farmed it on favourable terms.

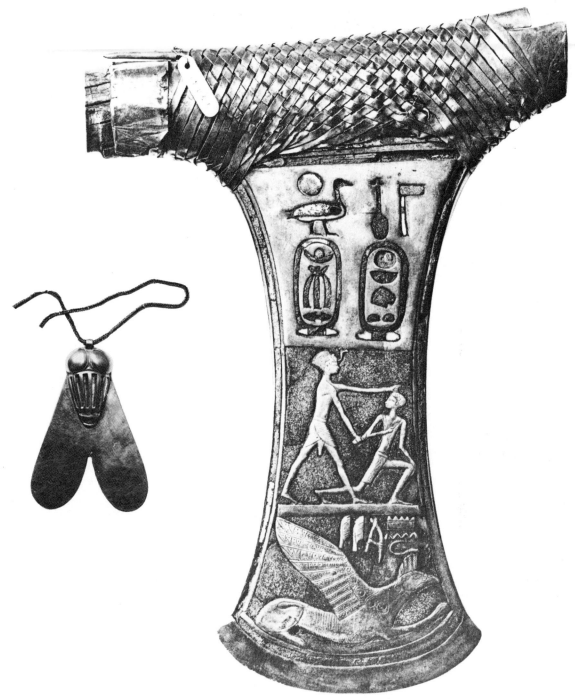

48
The massive gold fly of valour and the richly inlaid head of a parade axe from the treasure buried with Queen Ah-hotpe who rallied the Theban forces at a critical moment in their war of liberation against their Asiatic Hyksos overlords. It was appropriate, therefore, that such military decorations should have been awarded to her by her victorious son Ah-mose. He is shown on the axe-head wearing the new-fangled war-helmet and slaying one of the 'rebels' he had to defeat to secure the throne as the first Pharaoh of the XVIIIth Dynasty. Below, the Theban war-god, Mont, appears as a griffon.

49

Line drawing of part of the scene of the Battle of Kadesh carved on the walls of several temples erected by Ramesses II. The extract shows the Egyptian advance guard encamping within a shield palisade. Two captured Hittite spies are being beaten to extort the news that the Hittite forces, far from being at Aleppo, are at hand and about to descend upon the Egyptian armies as they are strung out in columns of march. Ramesses II, on his throne, summons his war council consisting of a vizier and general officers to discuss what should best be done in this crisis. His chariot, in the charge of a groom, stands ready for him to mount. At the top, Hittite chariotry attack his camp.

7   Artists and Artisans

All the evidence suggests that the Pharaohs held their artists in high esteem. Parennefer, for instance, who filled the office of Chief Craftsman under Akhenaten, not only had a large sculptured tomb at Thebes but an equally important one at Amarna and was sufficiently intimate with his king to be appointed his butler.

Kings themselves did not disdain to be considered as artists. Bek, the chief sculptor of Akhenaten, claims that he was taught by his king; while there is a passing reference to the designing by Tuthmosis III of a set of metal vessels. If the names of only a mere handful of Ancient Egyptian artists are known and pictures of them are very rare, and above all if we are unable to accredit nearly all the surviving works of art to particular artists, that is only what we should expect. In Ancient Egypt the artist worked under the same anonymity that prevailed in the early Middle Ages. He was considered primarily as a craftsman; and sculptors and painters are often shown at work in the same studios as joiners, metal-workers, potters and other artisans.

The individuality of the artist was of no importance in Ancient Egypt; what mattered was his ability to render faultlessly the ageless conventions, which he had imbibed from his master and would impart in turn to his pupil. But despite all the forces that operated to ensure that a statue or painting should repeat only the primal pattern, Egyptian art did move. The wonder is that it should change so much; and it is often possible for the expert to date a specimen to within a few years by its stylistic features alone.

How could such artistic changes come about in the conservative and traditional milieu of the Egyptian craftsman? The answer lies in the qualities of the designers of Egyptian art. In the early days when the centre of Egyptian culture was at the capital of Memphis, it was Ptah, the god who had brought all things into being by his creative utterance, who was also the creator of all artistic enterprises. His high priest bore the title of 'Greatest of Craftsmen', and it was such literate men who designed the buildings, their decoration and their contents. They it was who guided the hands of the builders, stonemasons, painters, jewellers, joiners and other artisans who made and embellished the works that they conceived. Such humbler craftsmen were isolated in workshops attached to the palaces, the houses of the great feudal lords, or the temples of the gods to whom nearly all their lives were dedicated. Only in their leisure hours could they make something for themselves or for modest patrons.

No better example of such an institution exists than the community of workmen who hewed and decorated the tombs of the kings and their families at Thebes during the New Kingdom. The excavation of their walled village has recovered many articles and documents which tell us much of their lives and work. Generations of artisans and their families lived in this village, their employment being hereditary. They enjoyed a fair measure of independence and self-government, but the vizier or a king's butler visited the site from time to time to inspect progress and to listen to any requests or complaints. During the XXth Dynasty these were not infrequent and mostly concerned irregularities in the supply of their rations. When protests had no effect the workmen downed tools. A strike in the last years of Ramesses III caused especial consternation.

The workmen were paid in kind, though payments of silver are also recorded at the beginning of a new reign. Their rations consisted of emmer wheat and barley, for making the staple bread and beer. The manual workers were given more generous allowances than the clerks and porters. In addition they regularly received vegetables and fish and a supply of wood for fuel. Occasionally, certain bonuses in the form of salt, wine, sweet beer and other luxuries were distributed.

A considerable force of labourers was detailed to provide commodities and services for them. There was also a police force for guarding the tombs, particularly those under construction. The gangs worked a ten-day week, living and sleeping in roughly built huts near the tomb they were preparing. On their rest days and the many feast days they returned to their homes in the village. In view of the popular idea that the monuments of Ancient Egypt were built only by the blood and sweat of expendable slaves, it is disappointing to learn that these artisans worked for four hours in the morning before knocking off for a meal and a nap. The rest of their working day consisted of another four-hour stint in the afternoon. Even so, absentee-ism was common.

---

50 (right)
Quartzite stela of Bek and his wife Taheret, now in Berlin. Bek served Akhenaten as his chief sculptor, just as his father had served Amenophis III. He claims that he was taught by the king and was his favourite, by which he probably means that he carried out the peculiar ideas that Akhenaten held about the way he should be represented. Bek was almost certainly responsible for the impressively disturbing colossi that he carved for the temple that Akhenaten raised at Karnak (plate 56). Here he has carved his own figure with the fashionable distortion of his royal patron's pronounced paunch.

51 (above)
Part of the workshops of the King's sculptors Neb-amun and Ipuky from the painting in their tomb at Thebes. They were not only sculptors but scribes, well versed, like the earlier sculptor Iritisen in 'the sacred books' which may have been the pattern books preserving the canons stored in some of the temple libraries. They must have been familiar with, if not proficient in, all the techniques employed by the various craftsmen under their charge. Thus Neb-amun, not visible on the left, inspects a jewelled collar, armlets and bracelets brought to him on a tray for approval. Other jewels are being prepared by lapidaries who also inlay a casket. Metalworkers chase a gold vessel and sphinx, while others planish gold vessels on stakes. Above, a scribe weighs out an allocation of gold using a bronze bull's head weight, and joiners make and assemble a wooden shrine.

52 (left)
Line drawing of a painting in the tomb of the Vizier Rekh-mi-re showing part of the workshops of the temple of Amun at Thebes. In the top register leather-workers are preparing skins while others cut out and sew sandals. In the middle register joiners using adzes, saws, chisels, rubbers and a bow-drill are making a column, box and bed. In the bottom register metalsmiths are raising large vessels on a wooden stake using pebbles as hammers, while another squats at his furnace with blow-pipe and tongs. Three men under the supervision of a scribe carry bronze ingots captured in Asia by Tuthmosis III for casting the leaves of two doors of the temple. All these different craftsmen are happily at work in the same studio.

53 (above)
Line drawing of a relief in the tomb of Huya at Tell el-Amarna showing Yuti, the chief sculptor of the dowager Queen Tiye, at work in his studios attached to the workshops of her palace. The care with which this small scene has been carved in the friable limestone, the over-large portrait head of Yuti and the repetition of his name, arouse the strong suspicion that this is the work of Yuti himself and the second occurrence of his name is his signature. He squats on a stool to put the finishing touches to the painting of a statue of Beket-aten, the Queen's daughter and a sister of Tut-ankh-amun. Other sculptors are at work shaping the leg of a chair with an adze, or carving heads with chisels, similar to the box-wood example in plate 55.

54 (right)
The men who directed the craftsmen and ensured that both the continuity and the innovations of Egyptian art were achieved under proper authority were the literate designers. In the earliest days when the centre of culture was at Memphis, it was the city god Ptah, 'the Creator who had made things with his two hands as solace for his mind', who was regarded as the patron of all artistic enterprises. His high priest bore the title of 'Greatest of Craftsmen' even as late as Roman times. One of a line of such men was Ranofer who was responsible for the making of this painted limestone statue carved about 2500 BC, which is among the masterpieces of Egyptian art.

55 and 56 (left)
This box-wood head in the realistic style of the last years of the reign of Amenophis III, with the eyes inlaid in coloured glass and the ear-ring in gold and lapis lazuli, is usually identified as Queen Tiye. It was therefore probably carved under the supervision of her chief sculptor, Yuti (plate 53). *Left*, Upper part of a colossal limestone statue of Akhenaten from the destroyed temple to the Aten at Karnak. This impressively distorted portrait could only have been carved at the instigation of the King himself, probably by his sculptor Bek (plate 50). Both pieces are rare examples in Egyptian art of work that can be credited with probability to particular artists.

57 (above)

The ruins of the workmen's village, 'The Place of Truth on the West of Thebes', where generations of craftsmen employed on making the royal tombs at Thebes lived from about 1500 to 1085 BC. The houses were built in groups and share party walls, the lower courses being of rough blocks of limestone. The upper parts and subsidiary walls were built of mud-brick and plastered with mud. The houses were one storey high and included a reception room leading into a higher living room lit by grilled openings, the ceiling supported by one or two columns resting on stone bases. From this room one door led into the bedroom and another into a passage giving access to the kitchen and to a staircase leading to the roof where so much of the daily life was spent.

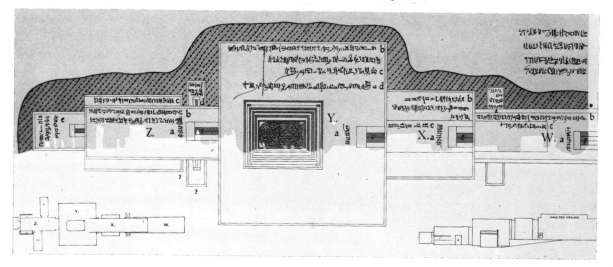

58 (above)

The workmen on the royal tombs followed a hereditary calling, the·eldest son usually taking the place of his father. The post of secretary to the community, for instance, was in the hands of six successive members of the same family. The secretary had to keep a diary recording the amount of work done each day, the names of absentees and the reasons for their failure to report. His reports were submitted to the Vizier who was thus kept informed of progress during the intervals between his visits. Such a record is contained on the above ostrakon which has been put together from several fragments. It records entries in the last months of King Sethos II on the right and the first year of his successor, Siptah. The regnal year changes abruptly from Year 6, first month of Winter, day 29 to Year 1 of the new reign; when high officials come to report 'the falcon has flown to the horizon,' i.e., Sethos II is dead.

59 (left)

Part of a papyrus in the Turin Museum showing the architect's plan of the tomb of Ramesses IV, with a modern restoration and drawings of the plan and elevation of the actual tomb by Howard Carter. The entries name the various chambers and corridors of the tomb and report the state of work done in them. The red granite sarcophagus with a recumbent figure of the King on the lid is surrounded by shrines and a pall-support similar to the arrangements made for Tut-ankh-amun. It was the duty of the scribe to see that the architect's plan was followed according to his measurements and instructions and to enter on it the state of completion. In this he was assisted by the foremen of the two gangs into which the workmen were divided.

60

The most notable of the sculptors' studios excavated at Amarna is the workshop of Tuthmose, the chief sculptor and favourite of Akhenaten. The famous painted bust of Queen Nefertiti has been accredited to him, though it is perhaps more likely to have been made by her chief sculptor whose name is unknown to us. A number of plaster studies have also survived which are so realistic that they have been identified as life or death masks. This head of Akhenaten, however, is clearly a cast from a master statue, as the fragment of the Blue Crown in front of each ear shows, made to be sent as a pattern to the various sites where statues of the King were being carved.

8 Scientists and Technologists

Science, as we understand it, is the study of basic principles from observed facts and their formulation into natural laws. This kind of scientific speculation would have seemed to the Ancient Egyptians to be presumptuously inquiring into the mysteries of the gods. They had, indeed, a kind of science but it differed markedly from that which is understood by the term today. They had collected a body of wisdom as the result of careful observation, the exercise of trial and the correction of error. With this knowledge they could solve the practical problems of everyday life.

As an example of Egyptian science we may instance mathematics. Various texts reveal that by the end of the third millennium BC the Egyptians had developed a respectable system of arithmetic and geometry, but since most of their learning was transmitted verbally from one adept to his pupil as a mystery, we have no means of assessing the full extent of their theoretical knowledge.

It is, however, extremely doubtful whether they were capable of doing more than solve problems connected with such matters as the distribution of rations or seed corn, the measurement of fields and the estimating of crop-yields for taxation purposes, the number of bricks required to build a given structure, and the number of men necessary to perform different kinds of labouring work. Nevertheless the inventiveness of the Ancient Egyptians produced effective results despite the absence of any spirit of scientific inquiry. The paper made from papyrus which they developed in the fourth millennium BC was still being produced in the eleventh century AD. Another substance that was greatly prized in the ancient world was lapis lazuli. The only source of the supply was centred in Afghanistan from whence it was exported all over the ancient Near East even as far as Egypt. At an early age, probably by about 2700 BC, the Ancient Egyptian had invented a calcium-copper silicate which closely imitated this most desirable but rare and expensive stone. He was able to mould this artificial substance into various objects. 'Egyptian Blue' as it is called was also powdered and used as a pigment, being exported to Italy as late as the seventh century AD.

His technology in fact, as distinct from his science, could accomplish enterprises that in recent times have fully challenged the ingenuity and resources of the modern world. As an example of this we may take the erection of large obelisks, which the Egyptians successfully achieved at least by the beginning of the second millennium BC. During the last century the French, British and Americans removed large obelisks from Egypt for erection elsewhere. The carrying out of these missions, using such modern devices as large compound shears, pulleys, capstans, hydraulic rams and jacks, was considered in each case as a notable achievement. A passage in an ancient papyrus, in which one scribe challenges another to calculate the number of men needed to transport a huge obelisk, 110 cubits long and 10 cubits thick, shows that such problems were well within the compass of the Egyptian Masters of Works.

The full technical achievement of the Ancient Egyptian is best appreciated, however, by examining one of his failures rather than his triumphs – the unfinished obelisk which still lies in the northern granite quarry at Aswan. It is 137 feet long and nearly 14 feet wide at its butt and if it had been extracted would have weighed nearly 1200 tons. Yet it was not because of an engineering miscalculation or a failure of nerve that it lies abandoned. The man who planned this colossal monument must have had every confidence that by his skill and calculations he could extract it from the quarry and erect it at Thebes or Memphis. It was a series of fissures in the lower bed of the granite matrix, which were only revealed as work progressed, that obliged the engineers to abandon their task. Their knowledge and experience were such that they knew that if they attempted to erect an obelisk of this size with such flaws, it would inevitably break in the middle.

The pounding of these great monuments from their beds of granite at Aswan, their removal on sleds to the banks of the Nile, their loading on great barges specially constructed for the purpose, their transport by river, their unloading, and finally their erection within a restricted space, all presented the Ancient Egyptian with formidable engineering problems which he triumphantly overcame with the help of his empirical technology.

It is true that the unfinished obelisk, weighing six times as much as Cleopatra's Needle on the Thames Embankment, was never moved from its quarry; but monuments just as heavy, such as the fallen colossus of Ramesses II in his mortuary temple, were successfully hewn and erected.

---

61 (right)
The red-granite obelisks of Tuthmosis I and Queen Hatshepsut still standing before the IVth and Vth Pylons in the temple of Amun at Karnak. Originally each obelisk had a partner. All four were erected within a narrow space by means of brick-ramps. The Queen's obelisk is $97\frac{1}{2}$ feet high and weighs 323 tons. It is the tallest left standing in Egypt. An inscription on it declares that it and its companion were hewn 'from one block of hard red-granite without any patches or flaws'. The work in the quarry took seven months. The Queen adds, 'Let not him who hears this say, "It is a lie!" ... but rather let him say, "How like her who is truthful in the sight of her father [Amun]!"'

62 (left)

The unfinished obelisk still recumbent in a quarry at Aswan. To find a suitable mass of granite the Ancient Egyptians had to go down to a considerable depth. The stone was worked by heating it between walls of mud brick, drenching it and pounding the fractured rock with dolerite balls which occur naturally in the adjacent desert. Not only was the upper surface levelled by this means but two separation trenches were pounded out on either side. Thereafter the obelisk had to be undercut, a laborious task, until it lay attached to its bed at a few points. The galleries beneath were then filled with suitable packing while the supports were bashed away, so that eventually it lay detached on a bed of rubble within its huge trench.

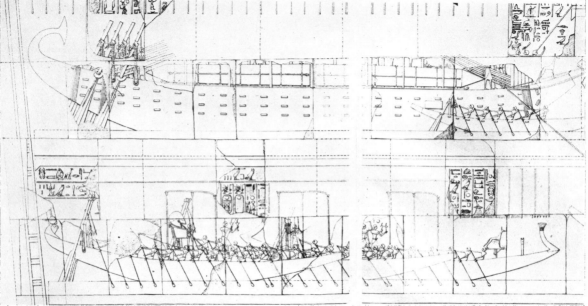

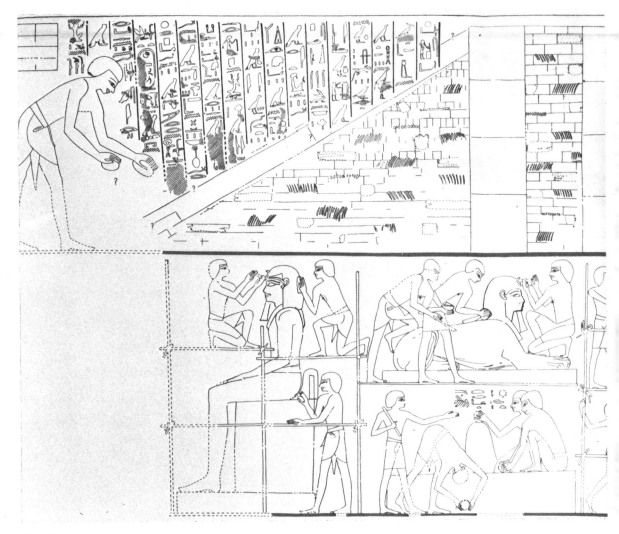

63 (above)
Line drawing of a painting in the tomb of the Vizier Rekh-mi-re showing the making of colossal monuments. In the lower register, sculptors are working on statues and an altar of Tuthmosis III. In the register above, what seems to be depicted is the building of a stone sanctuary, wall-blocks and the drums of columns being hauled up mud-brick ramps until each course is complete. The entire area is then levelled with rubble, wood, matting, stones and earth, ready for the ramp to be extended and the next course laid. When the 'topping out' blocks had been installed, the filling was removed and the stone dressed as it was exposed.

64 (left)
The obelisk had to be lowered down a sandbank by digging below its leading edge and using the levers to initiate a rolling motion like that of a cylinder. About forty ropes $7\frac{1}{4}$ inches in diameter pulled by six thousand men would have been required to control the descent. It then had to be manoeuvred on to a wooden sled and mounted on a transport barge. This drawing of a relief in the temple of Queen Hatshepsut (plate 24) shows two of her obelisks placed end to end on their barge, but is probably merely fanciful and it is more likely that they were stowed side by side. Even so this enormous barge was strengthened by three rows of cross-beams and towed downstream to Thebes by three rows of oared tugs, nine in a row, each row being led by a pilot boat.

65

The Rhind Mathematical Papyrus in the British Museum written about 1600 BC, and other similar texts, reveal that by the end of the Third Millennium BC the Egyptians had developed a decimal system of numeration with which they could make arithmetical calculations involving complicated fractions with comparative ease and accuracy. They could solve problems involving two unknown quantities and had simple notions of geometrical and arithmetical progression using fractions. They were also familiar with elementary solid geometry and the properties of circles, cylinders, triangles and pyramids. Since they could find the area of a circle with tolerable accuracy by using a value of π of 3·16 they could also calculate the volume of a cylinder. They could also determine the volume of a pyramid or truncated pyramid. This page from the Rhind Papyrus deals with problems of triangles.

9 Man and the Gods

Every year the land of Egypt, parched with the summer heat, was submerged beneath the waters of the inundation. As the waters receded and the land emerged, first as a narrow spit of sand, the muddy wastes sprang into new life. Seeds in the ground germinated in the gentle heat of winter and soon an active population of tadpoles, insects and birds was inhabiting the vegetation growing on what had recently been an infertile hillock of earth sticking up above the water. This miracle of creation occurred each year in Egypt and profoundly influenced the imagination and thought of its people. This, they believed, was how the world began.

Egyptian creation myths all have in common this primordial ocean, the Nun, and the mound of earth that arose from it, but the other features of the story vary from place to place. This is hardly surprising. Egypt as a political and territorial entity did not arise suddenly but grew from very diverse human settlements on the banks of the river. Communities of hunters, herdsmen, cultivators and fishers, each with their local deity and beliefs, contributed their systems of thought, their explanations of the world around them. In step with political unification these ideas were assimilated into a theology which had nothing exclusive about it. One set of beliefs did not refute the others, since the ancient had a tolerant acceptance of all divine powers – even the gods of foreign peoples. In the great religious centres of Egypt, the prototypes of the universities of more modern cultures, thinkers formulated their doctrines and attempted a synthesis of the various ideas that were abroad; and this process was continuous in Egypt for the three thousand years of its life under the Pharaohs.

It was at Heliopolis, the centre of the sun-cult, however, that a theological system was developed which gained a wide and deep authority from the influence it exercised over the office of kingship. The primaeval mound at Heliopolis was a sand hill on which was a stone of pyramidal shape, the ben-ben. When the ben-ben was elevated upon a tree-pillar, the result was an obelisk on the top of which the demiurge Atum appeared on first emerging from the Nun. According to some beliefs, this manifestation was as a mythical bird, the Phoenix. The usual version of the doctrine taught that Atum, the Completed One, arose on the sand hill from Chaos and there copulated with himself as a result of which he spat out Shu the god of air and Tefnut the goddess of moisture, and from this pair descended two other divinities, Nut, the sky, and Geb, the earth, by normal processes of reproduction. Re, the active aspect of Atum, is represented not in the usual human form of the solar deities but as the disk of the sun. He early became associated with a sky-god Horus, who was manifest as a falcon and incarnate in the king. A composite deity Re-Herakhty, the Re-Horus of the Horizon, emerged from this fusion; and the Pharaoh, the living Horus, became first an incarnation of Re; but later the myth was sedulously cultivated that the Pharaoh had been begotten by Re upon the Chief Queen, and 'Son of Re' became an essential part of the royal titulary.

The close connections of royalty with the sun-cult led to its widespread influence over the whole spectrum of Egyptian religion and the identification of nearly every local god with Re. The sun-god traversed the sky by day in a special craft accompanied by a crew of gods. At sunset Re boarded another boat to sail on the waters that are under the earth.

There were other beliefs belonging to earlier strata of thought which were assimilated into the sun religion. Thus an earlier sky-cult concerned with star-worship was absorbed and the circumpolar stars 'which never rest' became the crew of the day-boat, while the stars that rise at various times in the east and are visible for part of the night before setting in the west, 'the unwearying ones', were the crew of the night-boat.

The position of man in this universe was clear. He shared it with the gods and was not there on sufferance. He had been fashioned by god in his own image.

'Well tended are men, the cattle of god. He created heaven and earth according to their desire. He made the breath of life for their nostrils. They are his images that have come forth from his body.'

The Egyptian universe, then, was created by a god whose manifold forms and activities kept it in a state of being. For the Egyptian view of creation was not that it had been completed when the universe came into existence but that it was a continuous process which had to be sustained by worship and cultic practices.

---

66 (right)
One of the three great ceremonial couches positioned in the ante-chamber of Tut-ankh-amun's tomb was in the form of a cow bearing the disk of the sun between her horns. She is Isis-Mehit, the great primordial ocean, the Nun, in which Creation began. It is in fact not a bed but a boat on which the dead King traverses the ocean of Mehit for his rebirth. To the prehistoric pastoralist roving over the North African savannahs as they dried up at the end of the Ice Age, the difference between life and death was water 'that begets all living things'. The illustration shows the head of the couch in the form of a cow, bearing the sun-disk between her horns.

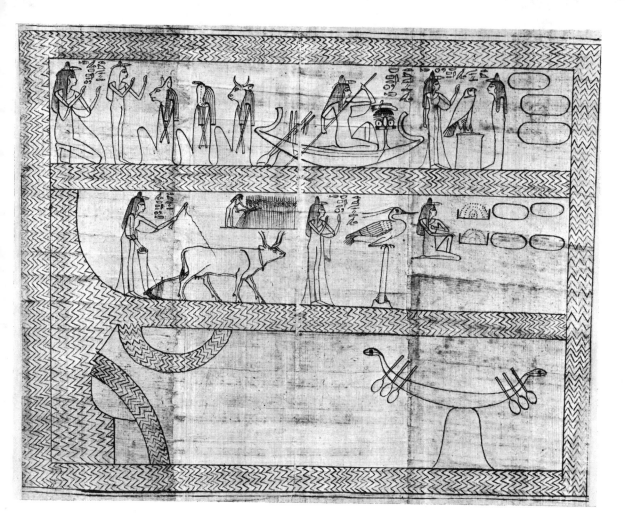

67

According to Egyptian belief, in the beginning was the inert water of the Nun containing all the germs of suspended creation within it. Something happened to begin the cycle of birth and as a result a mound arose out of the waters of Chaos which still surrounded the Egyptian universe. All the Egyptian creation myths have this feature in common but other aspects vary from place to place. At Heliopolis, the influential centre of ancient thought, it was believed that the Creator first manifested himself on this mound in the form of the Phoenix: and this vignette shows the bird alighting on the mound elevated on a pole, the obelisk.

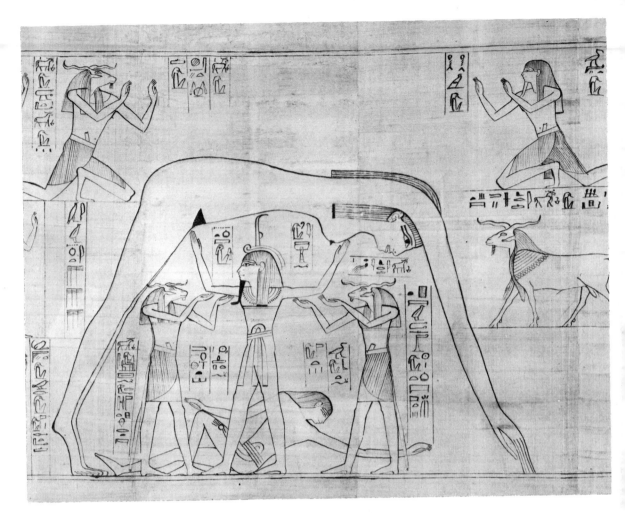

68

Another vignette from the same papyrus shows a further development in the Heliopolitan creation myth. The Creator, Atum, was the god of light who dispelled the darkness over Chaos and became a trinity with the first divine pair he formed from himself. These were Shu, the air, and Tefnut, moisture. From these descended another male and female pair, Nut, the sky, and Geb, the earth. Shu raised Nut from Geb and filled the vacancy between them. At night he lowered Nut upon Geb and from this coupling other gods were born including Isis and Osiris (plate 78). The scene shows Shu raising Nut from Geb assisted by ram-headed manifestations of the demiurge.

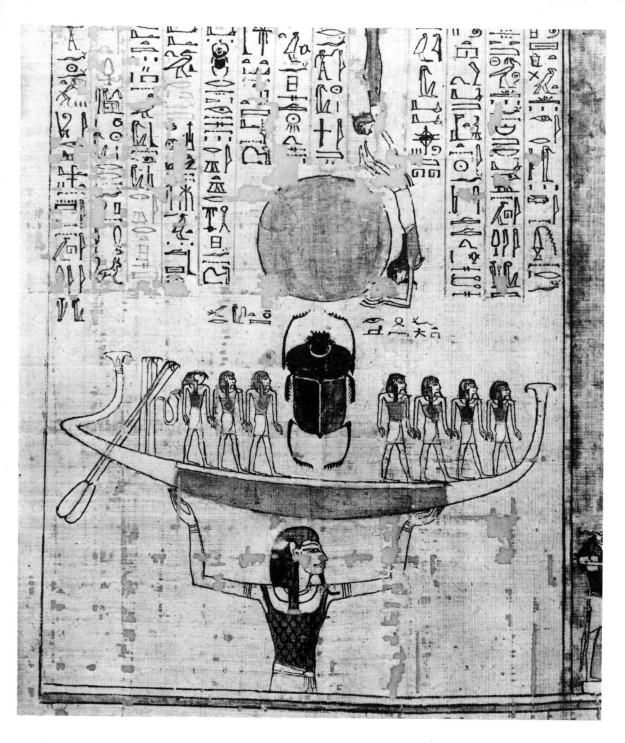

69
Re, the sun-god, reborn in the redness of dawn, traversed the sky by day in a special boat accompanied by manifestations of his power and by other gods. In this passage he had to contend with the cloud dragon Apophis (plate III), usually represented as a huge snake, but he always emerged triumphant even at an eclipse. This vignette, from the papyrus of another high-ranking Theban lady, shows the sky raising the day-boat with its crew to sail on the waters that are above the earth.

This neck ornament in gold and electrum, inlaid with semi-precious stones and coloured glass, is one which Tut-ankh-amun probably wore in life. The pectoral itself illustrates the universe as the Egyptian understood it. The moon in its aspects of a full disk, as well as a crescent, floats in a celestial skiff over the waters of the heavens in which grow lotus flowers similar to the one that opened from the Nun to disclose the sun-god (plate 15). They spring from the vault of heaven represented by a bar-like *pet*-sign supported upon the earth by sky-poles.

71 (above)

Another vignette from the papyrus illustrated in plate 69 showing, right, Osiris on his throne supported by his sister Nephthys and his wife Isis, all offspring of Geb and Nut. In origin, Osiris was probably a prehistoric fertility King who was ritually drowned in the rising Nile and buried beneath the primaeval mound where creation began and resurrection could follow. By historic times he was regarded as a former divinity, ruling over Egypt, who had been murdered by his evil brother Seth. Isis recovered the scattered members, reassembled them by surgical bandaging, revived the corpse and so posthumously conceived the son Horus who later assumed the throne. The appeal of this legend lay in the idea of a vulnerable god who had died like a mortal and been resurrected as a power in the hereafter. A promise was held out to all men who on death became Osiris (plate 78).

72 (below)

The manifestation of the dead man that could continue a ghostly life in the tomb was the *Ba*, represented as a bird with a human head as in this inlaid gold jewel from the mummy of Tut-ankh-amun. 'Thou shalt change into a living Ba and have power to obtain bread and water and air. Thou shalt take the form of a swallow or a falcon or a bittern whatever thou pleasest. Thou shalt cross in the ferry boat . . . thou shalt sail on the flood waters and thy life begin anew.' At nightfall the bird-soul, the Ba, returned to the tomb.

10 Death and Burial

Proper burial with due rites was considered by every Egyptian who could afford it as essential to the survival of his personality. The prehistoric Egyptian buried his dead in a crouching position in the dry sand of the desert as though awaiting rebirth. Above the grave was apparently heaped a hillock of sand and stones. By the early dynastic period such graves had become very much more elaborate, consisting of a complex of subterranean chambers and magazines lined with wooden planks and matting. The bench-like superstructure or 'mastaba' had developed into a large rectangular mass imitating the façade of a contemporary great house or palace. The idea of the grave as a place of rebirth was thus at an early date overlaid by the conception of the tomb as a kind of house, 'the mansion of eternity' as the Egyptians called it where, by magic, the deceased could continue a ghostly version of the life he had once enjoyed on earth.

From the belief that the *Ba*, or spirit, or soul, or ghost, could live on in the mansion of eternity like a twittering bird, there arose the vast elaboration of Egyptian funerary practices. When bodies came to be buried in sub-terranean chambers instead of simply in the desiccating sand, they had to be artificially preserved; and hence developed the practice of mummification, at first by dry-salting the body, in the same way as fish were preserved, after the internal organs had been removed and embalmed separately. With the embalmed dead were deposited the goods they had owned on earth and which they would require in their ghostly afterlife. Their chief need was for food and drink, and during the early dynasties a special niche was made in the superstructure of the tomb where food offerings could be laid by pious relatives of the deceased, who, like their modern descendants in Egypt, were accustomed to visit the tombs of the dead on feast days and there eat a meal in a kind of communion with the departed spirit of their ancestor. From this simple practice developed the great stone mastaba-chapels of the Old Kingdom with their courtyards, corridors, chambers and chapels decorated with painted reliefs of the deceased in all his worldly pursuits. The simple offering stela, with a picture of the owner seated before a table of food offerings, became a large false door through which he steps to partake of the daily meals. In periods of anarchy and transition, such as occurred at the end of the Old and Middle Kingdoms, the robbing of the tombs of former magnates or the lapse of their funerary endowments and a general impoverishment induced men to question the old tenets. On the return of new periods of high civilisation, however, the ruling classes revived with unquenchable optimism the belief that the tomb was the mansion of eternity. But after the New Kingdom, the tomb is often little better than a grave. The coffin with its scenes and texts became almost the owner's sole hope of immortality: the contents mattered less and less.

This change of view was not only the triumph of experience over centuries of wishful thinking. Other ideas of a more spiritualised existence after death belong originally to the cult of the dead king and manifest themselves particularly in two doctrines that steadily gained a wider recognition throughout the Old Kingdom. The first was that of the solar religion which under the influence of the priesthood at Heliopolis taught that the Pharaoh was the son of the sun-god who on death flew away as a falcon to the horizon to be assimilated to him who had begotten him on the Chief Queen. But there was also another cult which towards the end of the Old Kingdom began to spread with great rapidity and to influence the doctrines regarding the royal destiny. This was the religion of Osiris, a god who had died like a mortal and been resurrected as a power in the Hereafter, ruling over the dead, while his son stood in his place as the ruler of the living. Originally all such beliefs and practices belonged to the royal burial only; but they spread to an ever-widening circle of humanity until everyone who could afford a burial became as a king, an Osiris, on death.

But for all their apparent confidence the Egyptians really had very vague ideas of the next world and their views about it varied from age to age and place to place and were often in conflict. Death they regarded as a calamity which they hoped would not arrive until they had passed the ideal life-span of 110 years like that of the patriarchs of the Bible.

73

In this vignette from the papyrus of Hu-nefer in the British Museum the last rites are being performed. 'Invocation offerings shall be made for you and sacrifices made at your tomb stela.' The façade of the tomb is represented with its pyramidion above. Before the door is the round-topped stela. The mummy of the deceased is raised upright by a priest wearing the dog-headed mask of Anubis the god of embalming. The wife and daughter wail at the feet of the dead man despite his 'passing into bliss'. The ritual of Opening the Mouth (plate VIII), whereby all his faculties would be restored to the dead man, is performed by attendants under the guidance of a *setem*-priest wearing a leopard-skin robe. Below, a calf is sacrificed and the instruments of the rite are laid out on a table.

74 (left above)
A reconstructed predynastic burial in the British Museum. The dead man has been buried in the dry sands of the desert and his tissues have been preserved by natural desiccation. He lies crouched as though awaiting rebirth. Beside him are pots containing food and drink for his needs in the next world. Above the tomb there would have been raised a small mound of sand covered perhaps with pebbles, similar to grave-mounds made in Nubia until recent times.

75 (left below)
By early dynastic times such burials had become much more elaborate and enriched. The mound had developed into a bench-like 'mastaba' of mud-brick panelled with recesses to imitate the façade of a contemporary house. The deceased was laid out in an extended position, his shrunken tissues padded out with linen plastered and painted and dressed to imitate the appearance of a living person. He also acquired a coffin of stone or wood in the form of a house with doors and windows as in this sarcophagus of Ra-wer. The tomb has become the 'mansion of eternity'.

76 (above)
Despite the spiritualisation of the after-life in the Middle Kingdom, the monarchs of the New Kingdom and their high officials went to their eternal rest with even richer funerary equipment than before. This illustration shows the southern end of the ante-chamber of Tut-ankh-amun's tomb soon after its discovery. The material buried with these Kings was of two kinds—objects that they had used in their lifetimes and were therefore infused with their aura; and ritual objects designed to ensure their resurrection in the world of the sun-god as well as in the chthonian regions of Osiris.

77

The false door of Iteti in the Cairo Museum in which the deceased, carved three quarters in the round, steps into his tomb chapel to receive the funerary offerings. The deceased is shown in the essential scene of the relief seated before an altar, on which the ritual slices of bread are laid. A text above assures him of 'thousands of fowl, flesh, bread,' and other funerary offerings. The needs of the deceased are thus to be satisfied by magic also. Eventually magic in the form of prayer was to replace material goods in burial furnishings, and such prayers were to get even shorter. In this false door the invocation is still on behalf of the dead man; but a few centuries later, in the Middle Kingdom, the funeral offerings are petitioned for the *spirit* of the deceased.

78 (above left)
A wooden tray made in the form of the god Osiris, filled with earth sown with corn, and fitted with a perforated cover through which the seed could sprout. Such Osiris beds were put in some important tombs during the New Kingdom as a symbol of resurrection—the cycle of seed germinating to ripened head containing next season's seed. The Pharaoh, who in life had controlled the powers of nature for the benefit of his people, became identified with those powers on his death. As Osiris he was present in the growing corn, as the star Orion, as the inundation and the waxing moon. Man and Nature were as one.

79 (above right)
This effigy represents Tut-ankh-amun recumbent on the lion-bier upon which he will traverse the primaeval waters to his resurrection as Osiris, the ruler of the dead. He is accompanied by a falcon and a human-headed Ba-bird, symbolising what is expressed as early as the Pyramid Texts, that the Ba, or external manifestation of the King, is in the tomb while his spirit flies in the heavens. This latter concept is expressed in the prayer to the sky-goddess Nut inscribed on the effigy – 'cause me to be as the imperishable stars that are within thee', referring to an ancient belief that the dead entered the great circuit of the sky.

Epilogue

In the foregoing chapters we have outlined the means by which the natural
and human resources of the Nile Valley were employed in the fourteenth
century BC according to a system which had been developed at the dawn of
history and was gradually adapted to changing conditions with the passage
of time. Only once in its long history was this system radically altered; and
then for a brief interlude by King Akhenaten, the immediate predecessor of
Tut-ankh-amun, who introduced an intolerant monotheism which upset
the economic basis of Egyptian prosperity. Tut-ankh-amun, in a decree
which he issued early in his reign, describes the condition of Egypt at his
accession as being 'topsy-turvy' and promises to restore the morale and well-
being of his people by returning to those age-old principles which had
served them so well in the past, and which indeed were to prove equally
viable for the next millennium.

80
Pendant in gold, lapis lazuli, green felspar and
coloured calcite forming the rebus, 'Neb-kheperu-
re', the Son-of-Re name of Tut-ankh-amun.